# Preservation management for libraries, archives and museums

# Preservation management for libraries, archives and museums

Edited by
**G. E. Gorman and Sydney J. Shep**

LIBRARY

facet publishing

© This compilation: G.E. Gorman and Sydney J. Shep 2006
The chapters: the contributors 2006

Published by Facet Publishing, 7 Ridgmount Street, London WC1E 7AE
www.facetpublishing.co.uk

Facet Publishing is wholly owned by CILIP: the Chartered Institute of
Library and Information Professionals.

The editor and authors of the individual chapters assert their moral right to
be identified as such in accordance with the terms of the Copyright,
Designs and Patents Act 1988.

Except as otherwise permitted under the Copyright, Designs and Patents
Act, 1988 this publication may only be reproduced, stored or transmitted in
any form or by any means, with the prior permission of the publisher, or, in
the case of reprographic reproduction, in accordance with the terms of a
licence issued by The Copyright Licensing Agency. Enquiries concerning
reproduction outside those terms should be sent to Facet Publishing, 7
Ridgmount Street, London WC1E 7AE.

First published 2006
Reprinted 2007


*British Library Cataloguing in Publication Data*
A catalogue record for this book is available from the British Library.

ISBN: 978-1-85604-574-2


Typeset from editors' disks by Facet Publishing Production in 11/15 pt
University Old Style and URW Grotesk.
Printed and made in the United States of America by McNaughton & Gunn,
Inc., Saline, MI 48176.

# Contents

# About the contributors

**Gerrit de Bruin** is on the conservation team at the Netherlands National Archives, Nationaal Archief, and collaborated with René Teijgeler on the annotated bibliography, *Preservation of Archives in Tropical Climates* (2001).

**Marilyn Deegan** studied English Language and Literature at the University of Manchester, obtaining a first class honours degree. She was awarded a PhD at Manchester in 1989 for a study of Anglo-Saxon and medieval medical texts and herbals. She taught Old and Middle English at Manchester and at the University of Lancaster, before taking an MSc in Computation at UMIST (1989). She has been Manager for Computing in the Arts at the University of Oxford, Professor of Electronic Library Research at De Montfort University, Director of Forced Migration Online at the Refugee Studies Centre, University of Oxford, and is now Director of Research Development, Centre for Computing in the Humanities, King's College London. Her main research interests are: medieval literatures and cultures, in particular in areas related to health and disease; the use of new technologies in humanities subjects; and digital library development. Her publications include *The Politics of the Electronic Text* (with Warren Chernaik and Caroline Davis), *Beyond the Book: theory, culture and the politics of cyberspace* (with Warren Chernaik and Andrew Gibson) and, most recently for Facet Publishing, *Digital Preservation* (with Simon Tanner).

**Yola de Lusenet** has a degree in English language and literature from the University of Amsterdam. She worked for a number of years as desk editor for the Biomedical Division of Elsevier Science. She then took a job at a small independent publishing house specializing in academic publications in the fields of linguistics, literature and art, where her responsibilities included editing, production, promotion and acquisition and where she was Head of the Publishing Department for several years. Since 1995, she has worked as Executive Secretary of the European Commission on Preservation and Access (ECPA). Since 1996 she has also been the publisher of the Royal Netherlands Academy of Arts and Sciences, where the ECPA is housed.

**John Feather** has been Professor of Library and Information Studies at Loughborough University, UK, since 1988. He has an international reputation in the field of LIS education, and is the author or editor of many books and articles. In the field of preservation management these include *Preservation and the Management of Library Collections* (for Facet Publishing, 2nd edn, 1996), and, with Graham Matthews and Paul Eden, *Preservation Management: policies and practices in British libraries* (1996). He edited *Managing Preservation for Libraries and Archives: current practice and future developments* (2004), and, with Graham Matthews, *Disaster Management for Libraries and Archives* (2003).

**Mirjam Foot** is Professor of Library and Archive Studies at University College London, where she teaches 'Historical Bibliography, Preservation' as part of the 'Collection Management' course, and also 'Advanced Preservation'. She teaches a session on 'History of bookbinding: late middle ages/early modern period' for a Cambridge History MPhil Programme, and also 'Western Book Structures' in the 'History of the Book' MA programme at the School of Advanced Study, University of London. She teaches regular summer schools, both in London (Institute of Paper Conservation) and at the University of Virginia (Rare Books School), Charlottesville. She is a Past President of the Bibliographical Society, and a former Vice President and Council Member of the Society of Antiquaries of London. She chairs the

Bibliographical Society's Publications and Library committees, and from 2005 is editor of the Bibliographical Society's monographs. She sits on the Council of the Bibliotheca Wittockiana, Brussels, and on the Council of the Association Internationale de Bibliophilie. She has published extensively on the history of bookbinding, the history of decorated paper and on a number of preservation topics.

**Dr Helen Forde** is a professional archivist who has worked in local authority, private and most recently national archives. She was Head of Preservation Services at the UK National Archives (TNA) until 2001, and prior to this had been in charge of both the Library and the Museum at TNA. She now works as an independent consultant on archives. She lectures on preservation management at the School of Library, Archive and Information Studies, University College London, and is a regular speaker and organizer at training sessions and conferences on preservation both in Europe and internationally. She has worked extensively with the International Council on Archives (ICA) and has written numerous reports on archival preservation in many different countries. She is Vice-President of the UK Society of Archivists, Chairman of the East Midlands Museums, Libraries and Archives Council, vice-chairman of the Lincoln Cathedral Library Committee, a Trustee of the Marc Fitch Fund and the British Postal Museum and Archive, and a member of the Northamptonshire Archives Panel and the Museums, Libraries and Archives Council Designation Panel. Her publications cover a wide range of preservation and related issues.

**Dr G. E. Gorman** is Professor of Library and Information Management in the School of Information Management at Victoria University of Wellington. He is the author or co-author of more than a dozen books and more than 100 refereed journal articles. He is also editor of *Online Information Review* (Emerald), Associate Editor of *Library Collections, Acquisitions and Technical Services* (Elsevier), a member of the editorial boards of several other journals, and currently Chair of the Regional Standing Committee for Asia and Oceania of the International Federation of Library Associations (IFLA).

**David Grattan** is Manager, Conservation Processes and Materials Research at the Canadian Conservation Institute/Institut Canadien de Conservation. From 1996 to 2002, he was Chair of the ICOM Committee for Conservation (ICOM-CC), the largest of ICOM's International Committees, and continues to be heavily involved in the International Council of Museums. He delivered a paper at the ICOM Seoul 2004 conference on 'The challenge of the preservation of intangible heritage: the importance of electronic media'.

**Frank Ligterink** is a physicist and paper conservator at the Netherlands Institute for Cultural Heritage, Instituut Collectie Nederland.

**John Moses** is Native History Researcher of the Canadian Ethnology Service, and Conservator, Collections Management and Planning Division, Research and Collections Branch of the Canadian Museum of Civilization/Musée Canadien des Civilisations. He delivered a paper at the ICOM Seoul 2004 conference on 'Museums, aboriginal communities and the role of the conservator'.

**Dr Henk J. Porck** is Conservation Scientist, Department of Library Research at the Koninklijke Bibliotheek, National Library of the Netherlands and Curator of the Historical Paper Collection. He specializes in paper conservation, history and standards, and produced the *Preservation Science Survey: an overview of recent developments in research on the conservation of selected analog library and archival materials* (2000) with René Teijgeler. He spoke on 'Conservation Science: The Balance between Supply and Demand', at the IFLA Glasgow 2002 conference workshop 'Conservation Research and its Implementation in Libraries Worldwide'.

**Dr Bob Pymm** is a lecturer in the School of Information Studies, Charles Sturt University. Previously he was Manager, Collection Development at Australia's National Film and Sound Archive. For the past 20 years he has worked with audiovisual collections. He has published and taught in this area, as well as in the related areas of popular culture and libraries.

**Barbara Reed** has a distinguished reputation in archives, records and electronic document management in Australia and overseas. She is a Fellow of the Australian Society of Archivists, Director of The Recordkeeping Institute, Chair of the International Standard on Records Management, member of the Records Continuum Research Group, and member of the Archiving Metadata Forum. She has held academic positions at Monash University and the University of New South Wales, and is currently in demand as an appraiser and consultant to industries, including federal and state government, local government, small businesses, large corporations, statutory authorities and professional associations.

**Steph Scholten** received an MA in Art History from the Universiteit van Amsterdam in 1990. For two years he also studied public administration there. He became a qualified gold and silversmith in 1984. From 1988 he worked at the Dutch Ministry of Education, Culture and Science. For four years (1993-1997) he was one of the project managers for the famous Deltaplan project for the preservation of cultural heritage. During this time he commissioned and financed conservation research programmes. He was one of the co-founders of the Netherlands Institute for Cultural Heritage, which he joined in 1997, first as policy advisor and from 2000 to 2002 as head of the conservation research department at ICN. While at ICN he was responsible for the design and funding of a number of national and international conservation research projects for paper collections. He is now deputy director and collections manager at the National Museum of Antiquities in Leiden.

**Dr Sydney J. Shep** is Senior Lecturer in Print and Book Culture at Victoria University of Wellington and the Printer at Wai-te-ata Press, a letterpress teaching laboratory, research facility and fine press printing house. Her published research includes topics in New Zealand print culture, bibliography and book culture, paper history, typography and design, communication technologies and historic media forms. She has appeared as invited speaker at conferences of the Australian Institute for the Conservation of Cultural Materials, the New Zealand Professional Conservators' Group, and the Canadian Conservation Institute, and helped develop the University's Preservation Management course for its Master of Library and Information Studies programme.

**René Teijgeler** started his academic career studying sociology and social psychology at Utrecht University. In 1988 he was appointed teacher in bookbinding and graphic techniques at the Amsterdam School of Printing. He completed his education as a book and paper conservator at the State School for Conservators in 1993, and was appointed conservator at the Koninklijke Bibliotheek in The Hague. He continued his academic training in anthropology at Leiden and Utrecht University, and obtained an honorary degree in 1996. His research projects in preservation concentrated on the tropics in general and non-Western manuscripts in particular. He has studied writing materials from South and Southeast Asia, and was involved in a research project on Indonesian writing materials at Leiden University. In 1997 he started the consultancy firm Paper in Development and has since advised many projects in developing countries on preservation, papermaking, and book production. With Henk J. Porck, he co-authored *Preservation Science Survey: an overview of recent developments in research on the conservation of selected analog library and archival materials* (2000) and wrote an annotated bibliography, *Preservation of Archives in Tropical Climates* (2001) with the co-operation of Gerrit de Bruin, Bihanne Wassink and Bert van Zanen. He is currently working on the war's frontline with other museum, archive and library professionals advising on the reconstruction of Iraq's cultural heritage.

# Introduction

Forty years ago, on 4 November 1966, the River Arno in Florence burst its banks. In the days, weeks, months and years that followed, the fundamentals of book and paper conservation science were rewritten and new disciplines were forged: disaster management, preservation conservation and preservation management. This watershed moment, so to speak, has since been joined by spectacular episodes of cultural genocide. The 1992 burning of the National Library in Sarajevo, as well as the 1991 bombing campaign against the medieval city of Dubrovnik by Slobodan Milosevic's Serb nationalists, bore witness to the attempted erasure of Bosnian and Croatian ethnic identity. The Taleban's demolition of the Bamiyan Buddhas in 2001 destroyed 17 centuries of Afghan pre-Islamic sacred cultural heritage. The opportunistic looting of Baghdad's National Museum and the torching of the National Library and Archives in 2003 provoked international outrage, particularly as the invading forces did nothing to prevent the removal, destruction, sale, or relocation of cultural property.

However, there have been quieter revolutions to counterpoint the drama of flood, fire and war. Identification of the brittle books and slow fires syndrome drew attention to the dangers of self-consuming heritage artefacts and led to the formation of the Commission on Preservation and Access. From 2000, the highly publicized showdown between Nicolson Baker and the library and archive communities galvanized public thinking about the immanence of the original. Most recently, the global turn to digitization has forced scholars, collectors, curators and institutions to rethink and restructure their primary modes of operation.

Preservation management now sits at the top of the agenda for memory institutions around the world. It is a topic of ongoing debate as collection development strategies, policies and practices are negotiated between libraries, museums, archives, funding agencies and governments. Historically separate cultural institutions are now converging to share limited resources, develop compatible ideologies and co-ordinate distributed collections. In this climate, preservation and access are twin sides of the same coin: curatorial responsibilities are enhanced; the public is empowered.

The eleven essays in this volume chart the diversity of preservation management in the contemporary information landscape. Themes range from policy and planning to the challenges of new media and digitally born material, and from issues surrounding intangible cultural heritage materials in an indigenous setting to the status of the artefact in the electronic environment. Dynamic new approaches to conservation research are discussed as well as reconfigured understandings of the social contract in publicly funded institutions. Insights from the battlefields of Iraq are coupled with speculations about new directions in the definition and nature of the collection itself. The authors are academics, practitioners and consultants in Britain, Canada, the Netherlands, Australia and New Zealand, and are connected to a much wider international network of professional associations and NGOs. They have been selected as much for their specific expertise as for the contribution they will make to the field of preservation management in the next 40 years and beyond.

John Feather opens with a sweeping, yet nuanced, overview of the key issues in managing documentary heritage today and in the future. In a densely populated world of artefacts, selection is a fundamental preservation strategy, determined by cultural policy and, in turn, influenced by a bewildering array of social, economic and political contexts and pressures. As a result, objects transmit their historical fingerprint, and collections are living ecologies, testifying to the past, illuminating the present, and interpreting the future.

Mirjam Foot focuses the discussion on libraries and archives, demonstrating the necessary and logical integration of preservation-led decision making into the standard repertoire of institutional policy and planning. She frames basic library and archive functions such as collection management, retention policies, access frameworks, security guidelines, risk assessment and disaster preparedness with an awareness and understanding of the preservation context. Preservation policy informs preservation strategy, which in turn generates institution-specific preservation programmes.

Indigenous property rights and the guardianship of intangible cultural heritage in institutional collections offer significant challenges to conservators and preservation managers alike. David Grattan from the Canadian Conservation Institute joins John Moses from the Canadian Museum of Civilization to probe the paradox of ephemera and the obligations of culturally sensitive collecting and curatorship. Using the example of the Dogrib Traditional Knowledge Project, they advocate the concurrent need to preserve and manage documentation about artefacts as much as the artefacts themselves. In particular, they argue that objects in an aboriginal context do not exist in isolation but are part of a complex network of other media manifestations and culturally specific rituals.

Marilyn Deegan contributes to the ongoing debate about the relationship between surrogates and originals. She examines the nature of analogue or digital surrogates from the perspective of the reader/researcher and responds to institutional concerns about rationalizing the retention of specific items in light of alternative formats. Particular issues such as the authenticity (as opposed to authentication) of digital data, and the type of information the object or carrier itself contains and transmits are addressed. By covering the spectrum of memory institutions, she demonstrates that libraries, archives, museums and galleries are all faced with difficult decisions as well as liberating solutions.

Closely related to the surrogacy debate is the policy and practice of reformatting and migration as foundational preservation strategies. Yola de Lusenet picks up the thread of object value versus informational value, and embeds it in a discussion of the frequently conflicting demands of preservation and access and the expectation of some form of perpetuity for heritage collections. Using a wide range of international examples, she argues for a two-tiered microfilm/digitization approach which overcomes resource constraints and unprecedented collection volumes. She also reviews reformatting strategies for photographic and audiovisual heritage materials.

Conservation is often considered the mere technical servant of a broader preservation philosophy or agenda. The Netherlands-based team of Henk J. Porck, Frank Ligterink, Gerrit de Bruin and Steph Scholten argue, conversely, that conservation research is an essential and equal partner in the development of a preservation programme. As part of a recent Dutch national initiative for the preservation of library and archival materials entitled *Metamorfoze*, they have developed a new analytical model for cost-benefit decision making. This valuation instrument quantitatively assesses three key variables or success factors – preservation, access and economy – and enables the objective setting of conservation research priorities.

Whereas much of the literature on preservation and access has been based on paper objects, documentary heritage covers an enormous range of audio and visual materials, both physical and virtual. Bob Pymm surveys traditional and emergent new media and shares the challenges inherent in preserving evanescent and multi-modal formats. He affirms that preservation management in these domains is resource intensive, requiring an ongoing engagement with and commitment to artefacts rather than a single solution executed just once.

Barbara Reed joins the discussion with an examination of the special preservation needs of the digitally born object. Technically new and particularly unstable, these artefacts have particular challenges that are only now being identified. Pioneering ventures such as the digital capture of the 1960 US Census data or the 1986 British Domesday Project demonstrate the fragility and obsolescence of medium and format. How we develop management strategies for digital cultural heritage resources is becoming increasingly urgent as technology continues to drive the shape of information sources, as the public demands unlimited and long-term access, and as issues of content re-purposing, ownership, metadata and authenticity take centre stage.

A case study from the war zone of Iraq forms the basis of René Teijgeler's observations about the urgent need for heritage management planning in advance of man-made disasters, as well as inventive solutions during armed conflict and in its aftermath. He surveys various international initiatives for the preservation of movable and immovable cultural property and documents a number of specific historical instances of illicit activities and breaches of international law. From his experience in the field working alongside other museum, library and archive professionals, Teygeler shares insights about safeguarding our cultural heritage.

Helen Forde muses on the social contract between publicly funded institutions and the end-user, noting that the inalienable right to information embedded in Rousseau-esque ideologies of Western democracies must be balanced with robust preservation management strategies. She suggests that the delayed response by institutions to honour such a contract in the name of curatorial care or collection management, and by users to exert their lawful rights, is slowly being recognized and rectified. Recent Freedom of Information legislation, various Truth and Reconciliation Commissions and large-scale digitization projects have redefined the nature and ownership of official archives, artefactual evidence and memory records; retrospective cataloguing, updated retrieval systems and multiple access points including exhibitions and community participation programmes are the resultant stewardship priorities across memory institutions.

Finally, the volume's editors fast-forward to consider the changing nature of collection management, including preservation management, in the 21st century, and the potential impact on the information community. As museums, libraries and archives pool resources and harness opportunities for collaboration through digitization activities and networked access, new models of collecting and new paradigms for imagining cultural heritage institutions are evoked.

Any collection of this nature is only as worthy as its contributors make it. In our estimation the authors who have shared their research in this volume represent the most current and forward-looking viewpoints in their respective fields, and we are well aware of the time constraints under which they work. All the more reason to be grateful for their contributions, which will stand the test of time for decades to come; thanks to these individuals, this work has achieved our original intention. Behind the scenes there are the usual suspects without whom such a work would never materialize – the staff at Facet Publishing for their continuing confidence in our endeavours, especially Helen Carley, Lin Franklin and many others; here in Wellington, Jackie Bell, our unflappable copy editor. Our thanks to all who have contributed to the quality of this collection; we retain for ourselves responsibility for errors or omissions.

G. E. Gorman and Sydney J. Shep

# CHAPTER 1

# Managing the documentary heritage: issues for the present and future

John Feather

## Introduction

The preservation of the documentary heritage has to be seen in the broader context of managing what we have inherited from the past in a way which will allow us to hand it on to the future. Documentary preservation makes sense only when we also take account of the preservation of objects, the built environment and created landscapes. But we cannot preserve everything, and indeed should not seek to do so. As a society needs and desires change, the political and social expression of its understanding of, and need for, its inheritance also changes. In responding to change, each generation makes its own contribution to the heritage of the future. How we decide what must be preserved, and how we then preserve it in a meaningful way, is the question which lies at the heart of preservation management. This chapter explores these complex themes as an introduction to the more detailed studies which follow, and in this sense serves as an overview to the entire volume.

## Heritage and culture

Heritage has become a growth industry (Ashworth and Larkham, 1994; Lowenthal, 1998). A combination of cultural tourism at a time of cheap and easy travel, and nostalgia at a time of profound social change, has made heritage a part of the leisure industries. In itself this is not new. The 18th century grand tourists, who were the distant ancestors of the customers of easyJet, were a cultural and economic elite. If the democratization of wealth and education has not quite made Venice, Agra and Bangkok into destinations accessible to everyone, it has certainly opened up horizons – both geographical and intellectual – which were inconceivable in earlier times. Yet as international travel has become more available to more people than ever before, there has also been a growing sense of the national dimension of heritage.

A large part of the contents of the museums, galleries and libraries of Europe and North America has been removed from its place of origin. Some of that removal was a result of the spoils of war; some was simple theft; some was by agreement between equal parties; and some, of course, was by entirely legitimate commercial transactions entered into freely by consenting buyers and vendors. It is impossible to imagine the Louvre or the British Museum or the Metropolitan without objects which were acquired through all of these channels and others. Yet, the demand for 'cultural repatriation' has been insistent, but has largely been rejected by the heritage institutions and their political masters (Adi, 2005; Lowenthal, 1998, 244-7). Indeed, there are fundamental questions about the nationality of 'national heritage'. The *Mona Lisa* was painted by an Italian (who normally described himself as a Florentine) working in France for a French king. Is it French or Italian? The Portland Vase is the aesthetic root of an archetypically English design of ceramic which goes by the name of a culture – Etruscan – which produced neither the vase nor its derivatives, and of which little or nothing was known to those who made use of that name. Is the vase Roman? Or Greek? Or Italian? Or English? Or all or none of these? (Walker, 2004). And are the cloisters of the cathedral of Elne French or Catalan? Or, since they have stood overlooking the Hudson River for most of the last 100 years, are they now American? Will the cloisters return to Roussillon before or after the Benin bronzes are returned to Nigeria? To pose such questions is to show the impossibility of answering them, and exposes the complexity of the demand for repatriation.

The documentary heritage is not exempt from these controversies. Even within England, there are those who have argued that the Lindisfarne Gospels should be sent from the British Library to a repository in the northeast where the book was made in the seventh century. There have been calls for the return of colonial records to the national archives of the countries which were constituted out of former colonies during the 1950s and 1960s. It has been argued that Islamic, Buddhist and Hindu manuscripts should be returned to more appropriate places than western libraries. And not all of these demands have fallen on deaf ears. In 2001, the Lindisfarne Gospels left the British Library to be exhibited at a gallery in Newcastle upon Tyne in response to insistent public demand (BBC, 2001). The issue has now been addressed differently, using an elaborate website developed jointly by the British Library and the North East Museums Libraries and Archives Council (2005).

Technology has also come to the aid of archivists and historians in Britain's former dominions and colonies. Thousands of microfilms have been made of colonial and Indian records from the British Library and the National Archives for sale or donation to the countries to which they refer (National Archives of India, 2005). Arguments about acquisitions which resulted from wartime depredations also continue. An independent adjudicator, whose decision was accepted by both the government and the British Library, ruled in 2005 that the Beneventan Missal should be returned to the Italian monastic library from which it was looted (probably by the Nazis) during World War 2 (Department for Culture, Media and Sport (UK), 2005). But this is not one-way traffic. Books and manuscripts, like paintings and other *objets d'art*, are subject to rules which can restrict their export. The acquisition by the Fitzwilliam Museum of the Macclesfield Psalter is only the latest high-profile success in retaining cultural property in Britain (Cambridge University, 2005; Kennedy, 2005).

What is it that constitutes this documentary heritage? How is it defined? And how do we define its nationality? What is our social and cultural duty towards it? And how do we fulfil the obligations which that duty creates? These are some of the questions which this chapter addresses, with the intention of giving a broader contextual framework to the more practical issues with which much of the rest of the book is concerned.

## Documentary heritage: defining the domain

In common parlance, a 'document' is normally understood to mean a piece of paper with text or graphics on it. Among information professionals it is now commonly used to mean any information carrier, including electronic and audiovisual media (Feather and Sturges, 2003, 144). Historically, a *document* was the written evidence required in a court of law or for administrative purposes. Indeed, it was precisely because of the requirements of law and government that the authority of the written word came to displace that of oral evidence; it then became essential to authenticate documents and to preserve them in accessible repositories (Clanchy, 1979). The formal dictionary definition is somewhat broader; the *Oxford English Dictionary* (*s.v.* 4) offers this: 'Something written, inscribed, etc., which furnishes evidence or information upon any subject, as a manuscript, title-deed, tomb-stone, coin, picture, etc.' Taking the two uses of 'etc.' to include printing and books, we have here a definition which takes in not only the contents of libraries and archives, and also those of museums and galleries, but also objects which are part of the built environment. The distinguishing element in the definition is neither medium nor format, but the fact of writing, inscription or symbolic or pictorial representation. The driving force of the definition is that this was a human creation intended to inform.

Figure 1.1 suggests a typology which will help us to define and locate those parts of the heritage which are in the domain of the heritage institutions: libraries, archives, museums and galleries. All three domains – built and natural environments, and artefacts – include information carriers, but different levels of interpretation are needed before the information can be retrieved and used. An 18th century building can be used to help us to understand social and economic history, just as a man-made landscape can give us insights into agrarian history or the history

**Figure 1.1** The heritage sector

of aesthetics. But these 'readings' are essentially interpretative, in a way that 'reading' an 18th century book is not, even though there is always an element of interpretation in the reading of text.

It can be cogently argued that a properly interpreted building or landscape is indeed a document. English Heritage, the British government agency responsible for the historic environment in England, defines the objective of its research programme as '[contributing] towards providing public access to, and appreciation and enjoyment of, the historic environment for this and future generations' (English Heritage, 2005a). The British Library, similarly but differently, acknowledges its public role: 'The value we bring is essentially three-fold: we are a critical resource for UK research; we underpin business and enterprise through our contribution to knowledge transfer, creativity and innovation; and we are a world-class cultural institution with a vital role as a holder of the national memory' (British Library, 2005a). At least implicitly, there is a suggestion here that the contents of the British Library are more immediately intellectually accessible to its audience, and perhaps less in need of the kind of research-based mediation which is implicit in the approach of English Heritage. The capacity of libraries, archives and museums to provide direct access to the documentary heritage is reiterated in the fundamental statement of the aims of the UK government body charged with direct oversight of them, the Museums, Libraries and Archives Council (MLA): 'Museums, libraries and archives connect people to knowledge and information, creativity and inspiration. The MLA is leading the drive to unlock this wealth, for everyone' (Museums, Libraries and Archives Council, 2005).

In that spirit, the first Annual Report of the newly constituted National Archives (formerly the Public Record Office and the Historical Manuscripts Commission) emphasizes its role in relation to the general public as well as to other archive institutions and the archives profession (National Archives, 2004). A similar sense of public service is found in the missions of archive services throughout the world. The US National Archives and Records Administration (2003) is explicit: 'The mission of the National Archives and Records Administration is to ensure, for the Citizen and the Public Servant, for the President and the Congress and the Courts, ready access to essential evidence.' The National Archives of Australia (2005) claims that it 'encourages community awareness and use of valuable Commonwealth records in its care'. Even the more old-fashioned European approach embodied in the legislation which governs the operations of the French Archives Nationales (1979) acknowledges 'communication' (perhaps best understood in this context as 'dissemination') of the contents of the archives as one of its roles.

In the museum sector, this public dimension is, as might be expected, even more explicit. Museums are far more than simply another group of attractions for the cultural tourist. Their heritage function is encapsulated in this statement from the British Museum (2005): 'The British Museum's core purpose is to hold in trust for the benefit of humanity a collection representative of world cultures. Central to this purpose is sharing the Museum's collections and expertise as widely as possible.' In these two sentences, the British Museum succinctly describes both the preservative and the interpretative functions of the institution. Or, as English Heritage (2005b) expresses it in its context: 'English Heritage works ... to conserve and enhance the historic environment, broaden public access to the heritage, and increase people's understanding of the past.'

Although the documentary heritage - our stock of textual and graphic information carriers - is the focus of this book, we should never ignore this broader context. We learn about the past not only from what contemporaries wrote, but also from what they built, what they wore, what they put in their houses, what they did to their gardens and from all the survivals, deliberate and accidental, which now constitute the heritage. There is nevertheless a crucial distinction to be made: a house was built to be lived in; the household accounts were written as a record. It is with the latter category - the consciously created information-carrying artefact - that the documentary heritage is primarily concerned.

## An accidental heritage?

A significant part of the documentary heritage was created for the future, but that is not to be confused with its having been created to continue to exist indefinitely. And even when indefinite survival was envisaged - and even more in the much larger number of instances where the possibility was not even considered – it does not follow that the medium or format will enable that objective to be met. Organized societies have typically taken the trouble to make records and to protect them. Some documents and artefacts indeed carry a great burden of symbolic significance, for example Sibylline books (although perhaps not the best example of a well managed preservation policy), Magna Carta, the Declaration of Independence. But what of the Rosetta Stone? It is one of the most important documents ever found and interpreted for the historian of ancient Egypt, for it unlocked an unknown script and the culture which that script embodied. It was certainly created as a record, but it was not created as a glossary (Parkinson, 2005). The use of a document created for one purpose as evidence for another is a common theme.

The Rosetta Stone, despite its origins, is for all practical purposes an *objet trouvé* as much as if it were the head of a Neolithic axe. Much of the documentary heritage, however, has not been 'found' in quite the same way, because it has never actually been lost. Nevertheless, we can characterize a good deal of the survival as being accidental. Why do some books from medieval English monastic libraries survive? And why these and not others? Essentially it is because they were not destroyed. Some were rescued at the time by antiquaries such as John Bale and John Leland. They were consciously trying to preserve the irreplaceable, but we know that they were frustrated by the difficulties they confronted, and were often forced into serendipity where they would have preferred systematic selection. Yet the very existence of much unique evidence for medieval English history, not least for medieval English libraries, is a consequence of this rescue operation (Graham and Watson, 1998; Wright, 1958, 152-6). Even official records are subject to the vagaries of chance. When the Public Record Office was established in 1838, it took responsibility for a vast array of records which had been kept in a variety of conditions (most of them bad), in more than 50 different places (most of them unsuitable) and with very different levels of care and understanding (many of them low) (Martin and Spufford, 1990). Yet it is these survivors which constitute the official record of the government of England and much else from the Anglo-Saxon times to the accession of Queen Victoria.

Accidental survival characterizes the origins of much of the documentary heritage, including some to which we now ascribe the highest historical and cultural importance. Despite the sense of the need to preserve key documents, the idea that this has a broader cultural function is a later one. Essentially, public heritage institutions as we know them today are a product of the Enlightenment, exemplified by the foundation of the British Museum by Act of Parliament in 1753-4. It was the first free state museum in the world, intended 'not only for the instruction and entertainment of the learned and the curious, but for the general use and benefit of the public'. It was thus one of the most potent acts of the Enlightenment and at the same time one of its greatest achievements, with its explicit commitment to 'general use and benefit' (Sloane, 2003; British Museum, 2003). It was from its very beginning intended to be a comprehensive, albeit necessarily representative, collection. Before the century was out, it had already acquired systematically collected objects from every continent as British scientists and sailors continued to explore the farthest parts of the earth. This was a new kind of heritage: a created collection with a cultural and political purpose.

Although this was a new way to create a museum, it was one which was already familiar to librarians. As the printed book became the predominant format for the dissemination of texts – a process substantially complete in western Europe by the middle of the 16th century – the creation of libraries to contain the vastly increased number of books was a recognition of their importance. Libraries were seen as very practical institutions. Some were perhaps designed to boost the ego of a ruler or the reputation of a city or a university. In itself this was a serious purpose, but even more serious was the purpose of those which were effectively intended as instruments of propaganda. The systematization of the Vatican library was designed to promote the Counter-Reformation (Battles, 2004, 74-81), and among the Protestant rebuttals was the re-foundation of Oxford University's Library by Thomas Bodley (Trim, 1998). Bodley was a sophisticated and widely travelled diplomat; he may well have known that a copy of every book printed in France had to be given to the Bibliothèque royale. Whether he knew it or not, he used his political muscle to negotiate an agreement with the London book trade which obliged them to give his new library a copy of every book they produced. In 1662, this agreement was embodied in law and extended to other libraries, beginning the long and continuing history of legal deposit in the UK.

Legal deposit of publications in national (and sometimes other) libraries, like the requirements made of officials and their departments to deposit certain classes of document in national archives, encapsulates the desire to *create* as well as to *preserve* the heritage. This consciously created documentary heritage has a purpose beyond itself. In post-colonial Asia and Africa, a national library and a national archive have joined other institutions as symbols of nationhood itself (al-Nahari, 1984; Brindley, 2002; Humphreys, 1988). Their advocates and their custodians only rarely pause to ask *why* this is so important beyond its symbolic value. The answer, of course, lies in the sense that the documents – whatever the medium or format – have some intrinsic value as carriers of information, opinion or advocacy, but that they also have an extrinsic value as evidence of culture in the broadest sense. The hundreds of millions of documents in the national repositories of the world constitute our collective inheritance, encapsulated in the title (and some of the activities) of UNESCO's *Memory of the World* programme (UNESCO, 2005).

It remains the case that much of the content of libraries, museums and archives is there serendipitously. Accidents of discovery and survival, together with changing cultural fashions and intellectual perceptions, have determined the survival of much of what is now available to us as our documentary heritage.

## Selection for survival

Behind the serendipity, however, there are powerful forces which drive the selection process. Some of these are indeed conscious and intentional. The original purpose of legal deposit was political: François I of France wanted to know what was being printed in his kingdom so that he could control it. In Bodley's private-enterprise version, the motive was religious and academic. In the legislative version which followed in 1662, the motives were more mixed, but the desire to make books available in more than one place (i.e., to help to preserve them) and the recognition of their fundamental cultural importance were among the motives. By the middle of the 19th century, Sir Anthony Panizzi, the inventor of the modern concept of a national library, was arguing the case for comprehensive and enforced legal deposit on the grounds of preserving the national culture for the nation (Manley, 1991). From the middle of the 19th century until late in the 20th, the development (which meant the enlargement) of collections was the predominant motive of librarians in almost all libraries. The underlying assumption, explicit in some university libraries, was that the collections would be preserved in perpetuity.

This comprehensive (if ultimately unattainable) aim was actually predicated on the usually unspoken assumption that there was a process of selection. It was selection for acquisition on the assumption that what was acquired would be kept. It was a principle which informed the development of professionalism in all the heritage institutions, and still essentially drives the work of archivists. They are ruthless in their selectivity, as any code of practice for the management of public records will show (see, e.g., National Archives, 2005), but the initial selection for acquisition is also typically selection for retention. Not all retention is permanent, even in archives, but it is carefully planned for all classes of records. In museums it is also typically the case that acquisitions will be retained, although only a small percentage of total stock will be on public display at any one time. Librarians have a more flexible attitude. Much is acquired on the assumption that its shelf-life will be short. Indeed, in some libraries - including but certainly not confined to nearly all public libraries - the assumption is that nothing will be permanently retained. In every case, the underlying principle is the same: when items are selected for acquisition a decision about their long-term preservation is already implicit in the act of acquisition itself (Feather et al., 1996, 30-7; Ratcliffe, 1984, 17; Smethurst, 1988).

For the managers of libraries, museums and archives, however, the policy issues go far beyond the moment of selection and subsequent acquisition. Even if a document is to be kept only for a brief period of time, some steps may have to be taken to ensure that it successfully achieves its intended life-span (Feather, 1996, 94-5). For longer-term retention or 'permanent' preservation, more extensive measures are typically needed, and complex typologies have been developed which will both assist the librarian in making retention decisions and in determining what steps need to be taken to ensure that such a decision is implemented (Harris, 2000). These decisions have significant long-term implications for the management of the institution, for its budgetary needs and commitments, for the services which it can provide to its users and for its need for facilities and systems. Underlying these professional issues, however, are the much broader cultural considerations which have been the wider concern of this chapter. To select an object for preservation or disposal is, in effect, to make a decision about how the future will perceive and understand its past. Yet we know that universal preservation is not possible. There are some documents which are simply not created for long-term preservation; perhaps the most obvious are newspapers, for which, despite the sentimental pleas of romantics (Baker, 2002), there are insuperable problems of physical preservation and resource management which can only be addressed by concentrating on content rather than form (McKitterick, 2002). There is no question that the documentary cultural heritage is in danger. But there are environmental, cultural, educational, political and economic forces which militate against even the recognition of this fact. Even when it is recognized, the scale of the problem can seem overwhelming, and the solutions unrealistic. When this is taken together with the radical changes in the culture of communication and processing of information, the most pessimistic view is that there are real question marks over our collective capacity to preserve what we have inherited and to enhance the inheritance of future generations (Stille, 2002).

## The digital dilemma

The rapid development of digital technologies in the last decade of the 20th century can already be seen to have wrought a fundamental change in cultural attitudes. The written and printed word, so long accorded a special and privileged place in the west's perception of itself, has lost its unique symbolic power (Willison, 2000). Since the mid-1990s, the world wide web has become the principal source of information for millions of people, and by no means only the young. Together with other digital technologies (especially satellite television and cellular telephone networks) it has transformed our knowledge and perhaps even our concept of the world in which we live. With instantaneous global communications, we are no longer dependent on human contact in order to achieve human intercourse. The social and economic consequences of this cultural revolution are only just becoming apparent, and some are far from being predictable (Castells, 2001).

For the custodians of the documentary heritage, and the managers of the institutions where it is held, the network society presents a particular dilemma, but also great opportunities. The dilemma lies in the nature of the digital product itself. At the simplest level, millions of words which would once have been printed or written are now put into the public domain in electronic formats only. This affects heritage institutions and their information professionals in virtually all of their activities. How are digital documents to be preserved? How are they to be selected for preservation? What is the role of institutions in the process? And what kind of institutions will they be? Answers are beginning to emerge to some of these questions. Legal deposit in the UK was extended to digital documents in 2003 (British Library, 2005b); it also exists, albeit in more limited form, in the USA (Copyright Office, 2005). The issues around digital preservation are not completely different from those with which librarians, archivists and curators have traditionally dealt. Intellectually, the same considerations will drive the selection of materials. But the technical issues are profoundly different, and are inevitably leading to greater collaboration between the heritage institutions themselves, internationally as well as at a national level, and between them and the private sector providers of digital objects and the technologies used to store and retrieve them (Bremer-Laamanen and Stenvall, 2003). The longer-term issues are understood in principle, but are only now beginning to be addressed in practice (Deegan and Tanner, 2002, 178–208; Muir, 2003). The parameters have been changed both by the fundamentally dynamic nature of digital documents (which some might call instability), and by the complete dependence on technology to store and retrieve them. These same documents, however, are accessible without ever visiting a heritage institution. Desktop access to information has become the norm. The heritage institution which preserves 'born digital' products will consist of servers and networks, not book stacks, store rooms, reading rooms and galleries. We shall be able to preserve far more data than has ever been possible before, provided we have the technical capacity to do so.

For existing heritage institutions, the issues are manifold. For national libraries and for archives, there is no alternative to becoming a digital repository, or ceding a part of the traditional function of the institution to a repository in another domain. For other libraries, there is the certainty that holdings will become even less important, and access even more, than has been the case during the last third of the last century. The danger is that the knowledge, understanding and skills needed to preserve the heritage from earlier times will be lost or downgraded. One solution to this – or perhaps more accurately one way to avoid the problem – is to move towards digitization of analogue documents. This is indeed being done on a large scale, and may well be the long-term solution to the problems of preserving the contents of both written and printed documents more economically than can be achieved by keeping the originals. But not everything can or will be digitized, and for three-dimensional objects it is a particularly unsatisfactory solution.

Nevertheless, it is the case that digital technologies offer unprecedented opportunities to heritage institutions and to the promoters of heritage preservation. The websites of the world's great libraries, archives and museums (some of them cited in this chapter) vividly illustrate what can be achieved with imagination and resources. We have not yet reached the point where geography is irrelevant – indeed it would be an economic disaster for the tourist industry if it were – but it is certainly the case that the institutions can open up their contents to more people and in more ways. The controversy over the Lindisfarne Gospels has not entirely ceased, but the presence of the book on the British Library website has certainly come close to solving the problem of access in a way which actually gives the user in northeast England (and everywhere else on the planet) far greater individual access than could ever be possible to the original documents (British Library, 2005c). Digitization does not 'solve' the 'problem' of preservation, but it has added another powerful weapon to the armoury of solutions.

## Conclusions: the future of the documentary heritage

Cultural heritage is for everyone. The physical heritage, especially perhaps the built and natural environment, is in some ways the most accessible, although even here access needs to be re-enforced, public awareness needs to be enhanced and the need for effective interpretation is paramount (Department for Culture, Media and Sport, 2002). The documentary heritage is, at least superficially, more accessible without expert mediation. Historically, however, it has been less accessible in other senses, certainly in archives and many libraries. Museums and galleries display and interpret their contents (or at least a selection of them) to the general public, and all have made real and successful efforts to reach out beyond their traditional audiences. For libraries and archives, the problem is different, although as heritage institutions they have much in common with some aspects of the presentation of museums. Using their websites to open their treasures to a wider audience has created a greater understanding of what they do, and its relevance to a society's understanding of itself. But at their heart, archives and research libraries are intellectual institutions with a public face rather than public institutions with a scholarly underpinning. For their managers, who are merely their temporary custodians on behalf of society, the central dilemma is how to preserve what has been inherited and to enhance that heritage for future generations. But this is more than an exercise in preservation. The museums have led where libraries and archives must follow. The documentary heritage needs to be made available and interpreted not to the few but to everyone. The duty to preserve is fundamental, but the duty to interpret is the ultimate objective.

## References

Adi, H. (2005) Offence Taken, *Museums Journal*, **105** (5), 14-15.

al-Nahari, A. M. (1984) *The Role of National Libraries in Developing Countries*, London, Mansell.

Archives nationales de France (2005) *Décret n° 79-1037 du 3 janvier 1979*, www.archivesnationales.culture.gouv.fr [accessed 14 September 2005].

Ashworth, G. J. and Larkham, P. J. (1994) *Building a New Heritage: tourism, culture and identity in the new Europe*, London, Routledge.

Baker, N. (2002) *Double Fold: libraries and the assault on paper*, London, Vintage.

Battles, M. (2004) *Library: an unquiet history*, London, Vintage.

Bremer-Laamanen, M. and Stenvall, J. (2003) Selection for Digital Preservation: dilemmas and issues. In Feather, J. (ed.) *Managing Preservation for Libraries and Archives: current practice and future developments*, Aldershot, Ashgate.

Brindley, L. J. (2002) The Role of National Libraries in the 21st Century, *Bodleian Library Record*, **17** (6), 464-81.

British Broadcasting Corporation (2001) *Tyne on Show: the Lindisfarne Gospels*, www.bbc.co.uk/tyne/features/gospels/gospels_on_show.shtml [accessed 14 September 2005].

British Library (2005a) *Redefining a Great Library in the 21st Century*, www.bl.uk/about/strategic/redefining.html [accessed 14 September 2005].

British Library (2005b) *Legal Deposit*, www.bl.uk/about/policies/legaldeposit.html#elec [accessed 14 September 2005].

British Library (2005c) *Online Gallery: turning the pages*, www.bl.uk/onlinegallery/ttp/ttpbooks.html [accessed 14 September 2005].

British Museum (2003), www.thebritishmuseum.ac.uk/enlightenment/theageof.html.

British Museum (2005) *The Museum in Britain/Partnership UK*, www.thebritishmuseum.ac.uk/partnershipuk/index.html [accessed 14 September 2005].

Cambridge University (2005) *Macclesfield Psalter Saved for the Nation*, www.admin.cam.ac.uk/news/dp/2005012402 [accessed 14 September 2005].

Castells, M. (2001) *The Internet Galaxy: reflections on the internet, business and society*, Oxford, Oxford University Press.

Clanchy, M. T. (1979) *From Memory to Written Record: England 1066-1307*, London, Edward Arnold.

Copyright Office (US) (2005) *Mandatory Deposit of Copies or Phonorecords for the Library of Congress*, www.copyright.gov/circs/circ07d.html#brief

[accessed 14 September 2005].

Deegan, M. and Tanner, S. (2002) *Digital Futures: strategies for the information age*, London, Library Association Publishing.

Department for Culture, Media and Sport (UK) (2002) *People Places: social inclusion policy for the built and historic environment*, www.culture.gov.uk [accessed 14 September 2005].

Department for Culture, Media and Sport (UK) (2005) *Spoliation Panel Rule that Beneventan Missal - Acquired in Good Faith by British Library - was Looted in Nazi Era and Must be Returned*, www.culture.gov.uk/global/press_notices/archive_2005/dcms047_05.htm [accessed 14 September 2005].

English Heritage (2005a) *Research Strategy 2005–2010*, www.english-heritage.org.uk/server/show/nav.8652 [accessed 14 September 2005].

English Heritage (2005b) *Who We Are*, www.english-heritage.org.uk/server/show/conWebDoc.166 [accessed 14 September 2005].

Feather, J. (1996) *Preservation and the Management of Library Collections*, 2nd edn, London, Library Association Publishing.

Feather, J., Matthews, G. and Eden, P. (1996) *Preservation Management: policies and practices in British libraries*, Aldershot, Gower.

Feather, J. and Sturges, P. (2003) *International Encyclopaedia of Information and Library Science*, 2nd edn, London, Routledge.

Graham, T., and Watson, A. G. (1998) *The Recovery of the Past in Early Elizabethan England*, Cambridge, UK, Cambridge Bibliographical Society.

Harris, C. (2000) Selection for Preservation. In Banks, P. N. and Pilette, R. (eds), *Preservation: issues and planning*, Chicago, American Library Association.

Humphreys, K. W. (1988) *A National Library in Theory and in Practice*, London, British Library.

Kennedy, M. (2005) £1.7m Keeps Medieval Book in UK, *The Guardian* (25 January), www.guardian.co.uk/uk_news/story/0,,1397620,00.html [accessed 14 September 2005].

Lowenthal, D. (1998) *The Heritage Crusade and the Spoils of History*, Cambridge, UK, Cambridge University Press.

Manley, K. (1991) The Book Wolf Bites a Bohn: Panizzi, Henry Bohn, and legal deposit, 1850-53. In Harris, P. R. (ed.), *The Library of the British Museum: retrospective essays on the Department of Printed Books*, London, British Library.

Martin, G. H. and Spufford, P. (eds) (1990) The Records of the Nation: The Public Record Office 1838-1938; *The British Record Society, 1888-1988*, Woodbridge, Boydell Press.

McKitterick, D. (ed.) (2002) *Do We Want to Keep Our Newspapers?*, London, Office for Humanities Communication.

Muir, A. (2003) Issues in the Long-term Management of Digital Material. In Feather, J. (ed.), *Managing Preservation for Libraries and Archives: current practice and future developments*, Aldershot, Ashgate.

Museums, Libraries and Archives Council (2005) *What We Do*, www.mla.gov.uk [accessed 14 September 2005].

National Archives (2004) *A New Gateway to British History*, www.nationalarchives.gov.uk/about/operate/pdf/entire_report_04.pdf [accessed 14 September 2005].

National Archives (2005) *Operational Selection Policies*, www.nationalarchives.gov.uk/recordsmanagement/selection/ospintro.htm [accessed 14 September 2005].

National Archives and Records Administration (US) (2003) *Ready Access to Essential Evidence*, www.archives.gov/about/plans-reports/strategic-plan/2003/index.html#mission [accessed 14 September 2005].

National Archives of Australia (2005), www.naa.gov.au/ [accessed 14 September 2005].

National Archives of India (2005) *Holdings: public and private*, http://nationalarchives.nic.in/holdings.html [accessed 14 September 2005]

North East Museums Libraries and Archives Council/British Library (2005) *The Lindisfarne Gospels*, www.lindisfarnegospels.org/ [accessed 14 September 2005].

Parkinson, R. (2005) *The Rosetta Stone*, London, British Museum Press.

Ratcliffe, F. W. (1984) *Preservation Policies and Conservation in British Libraries*, London, British Library Research and Development Department.

Sloane, K. (ed.) (2003) *Enlightenment: discovering the world in the 18th century*, London, British Museum.

Smethurst, J. M. (1988) The Relationship between Acquisition, Retention and Preservation Policies. In *Conservation and Collection Management: Proceedings of a Seminar at Loughborough University of Technology, 22–23 July 1987*, London, National Preservation Office, British Library, 11–19.

Stille, A. (2002) *The Future of the Past: how the information age threatens to destroy our cultural heritage*, London, Picador.

Trim, D. J. B. (1998) Sir Thomas Bodley and the Protestant Cause, *Bodleian Library Record*, **16** (4), 314–40.

UNESCO (2005) *Memory of the World*, www.unesco.org/webworld/mdm/fr_index_2.html [accessed 14 September 2005].

Walker, S. (2004) *The Portland Vase*, London, British Museum Press.

Willison, I. (2000) 'Massmediaization' of the Trade Book: an American export?, *Logos*, **11** (3), 139–43.

Wright, C. E. (1958) The Dispersal of Libraries in the 16th Century. In Wormald, F. and Wright, C. E. (eds), *The English Library before 1700*, London, University of London/Athlone Press.

CHAPTER 2

# Preservation policy and planning

Mirjam Foot

## Introduction

This chapter discusses preservation policy, strategy and planning for libraries and archives. It argues the case for a preservation policy, indicates how preservation is linked to a number of library and archive functions, and gives guidance for formulating a preservation policy. Planning for preservation programmes is based on such a policy, and criteria for selection for preservation and for priority setting, as well as costing and monitoring of programmes, record keeping and reporting, are discussed. A good basis for preservation planning is the assessment of risks faced by buildings and collections, both every day and in extreme circumstances. Finally, risk assessment is explained and a brief outline is given of disaster prevention and disaster management.

## Policy

A preservation policy is a plan of action for the safe keeping of library and archive materials. It is preferably written, but not set in stone: a living document, to be used, checked, and revised if and when the need arises. It states what needs to be preserved, why, for what purpose, and for how long. It differs from a preservation strategy - the management of all the tools and skills at our disposal to fight against damage and decay - which sets out how and in what order material is to be preserved.

For several decades libraries and archives have been aware of the need to have preservation policies, not only to raise and maintain awareness of preservation issues among staff and users, but also to bid for funds, to demonstrate that funds will be used in a responsible way and to long-term good effect, and to justify expenditure. Preservation policies are a visible expression of intent, they are signs of accountability, and they allocate responsibility to the governors, staff and users of an institution; they can explain why decisions are taken and why certain actions are or are not carried out; they are used to allocate funding, develop preservation strategies and plan coherent preservation programmes, programmes that add up to an overall useful result, taking into account the needs and benefits of the collections; they can be monitored and they form benchmarks against which performance can be judged.

## Aims and purposes of the library or archive

Before a preservation policy can be formulated, a number of issues need to be taken into account, the most basic of which are the aims and purposes of the library or archive to which the policy applies. There are a great many different types of library and archive, ranging from national institutions and large research collections to highly specialized libraries and archives, local record offices and public lending libraries. They cater for a wide variety of users, from academics, private researchers and business people, to casual visitors, children, and all those who want to be informed and entertained. They all have different aims and purposes, as well as different duties to their users. Their preservation decisions need to be guided by those aims and by the needs of their users. Different types of collections have different functions and are used in a variety of ways. They serve a multitude of purposes and it is the purpose of the collection that determines its preservation needs. The nature of the material itself is also of importance. A collection can contain original sources and secondary material, basic reference material and ephemera, in a variety of formats and consisting of all kinds of material, ranging from print on paper, or manuscript on parchment, in a conventional sewn and bound structure or in loose sheets, from maps, atlases, and sheet music, to globes, seals, scrolls, acetate film, slides and photographs, videos, CD-ROMs, databases, online electronic formats and many others. All these formats impose their own conditions; they need different strategies and demand different technical solutions. But the aim and purpose of a library or archive and its function determine its preservation policy, which should cover all formats and all media.

## Functions and activities of the library or archive

Preservation does not exist in isolation. It is linked to other library and archive functions and a preservation policy should take those functions and activities into account. All libraries and archives acquire or receive material, with the intention of making it available to those who want to use it and of keeping it, at least for some time. If we look at acquisition, access and retention in turn, we will see that they are closely linked to preservation. Acquisition decisions have an impact on preservation decisions, but they can also themselves be preservation decisions. If, for example, it is decided to acquire a text in hard copy rather than in paperback, on microfilm, or in electronic format, this will have implications for the preservation of such a text. If it is decided to acquire a rare edition relatively cheaply but in bad condition, this will imply a preservation cost. The purpose of an acquisition influences its preservation needs as well: whether a text is acquired merely for short-term use, to be replaced by a newer and more up-to-date version as soon as, or even before, it has worn out; whether it is acquired in the first instance for lending or for reference use on the library's premises only; whether it is acquired for medium-term heavy use, as so many university textbooks are, or mainly for long-term retention, to become the national archival copy. These are only a few possibilities, but in all these the preservation decisions will have to follow the purpose of the acquisition. The format in which a text is acquired also influences its preservation requirements. Different decisions have to be made following the acquisition of a well bound book printed on sound paper, of a much-damaged brittle late 19th-century publication, of a bundle of loose papers in different sizes and in varying condition, or of a set of newspapers, a collection of photographs or drawings, or a CD-ROM.

Acquisition decisions are often guided by the perceived needs of the user, those currently in need of consulting the library or archive, as well as those who may wish to do so at some future date. Both the way in which access to a collection is provided and the amount and kind of use that is made of it directly affect its preservation needs. Making good and detailed catalogues available online will increase use and thereby increase the need for some extra protection and possibly also for conservation treatment. On the other hand, catalogues help to define what is in a collection, thereby preventing users from asking for the wrong material and thus preventing unnecessary handling. Catalogues can also refer readers to surrogates, thereby safeguarding the originals, or at least limiting their use to those who need to see more than just the text. Library and archive materials can be used in many different ways. Direct, physical consultation on the premises, borrowing for reading at home or in the reader's place of work, reading a text in a surrogate copy or in the original, consultation online, or looking at books and documents displayed on exhibition, are all forms of use, which have a direct impact on the preservation needs of the material thus consulted. The concepts of access and use are important for most libraries and archives, many see these as their sole *raison d'être*, and many libraries consider the amount of current use that is made of their collections as an indication of their preservation needs. This presents no problems with heavily used material, which will need protection or treatment or both, to keep it in a fit condition to be used. But the converse of such an argument is a dangerous one and great caution is needed when low use is considered a reason for neglect. One day such low-use material may well prove vital for research, vital for the advancement of knowledge, and it is the library's or archive's duty to ensure that it is still available to be handled and to be used. The increasing tendency in many parts of the library world away from ownership and collecting in favour of the provision of access, reduces its long-term ability to fulfil the research needs of future generations. Moreover, thought must be given to whose responsibility it is to maintain such access.

Providing access to collections while preserving them for future use can be seen (at least for analogue material) as two conflicting aims. There are indeed kinds of access that defeat or prevent future use, in the same way as there are preservation methods that inhibit access. Nevertheless, such conflicts can be resolved and if the need for and the purpose of access are considered carefully, the dilemma between access and preservation is not quite so acute. For electronic material access can assist preservation. Such material does not deteriorate through use, while systematic access helps to check whether publications in electronic format are still usable.

Future use implies retention, another issue that is inextricably linked with preservation. In most libraries, unlike archives, acquisitions are not always made with a retention or non-retention decision clearly in mind. Often in a library the decision to keep an item in the medium term, in the long term, or even in perpetuity, can only be made once its usefulness in the short term has been proven and there is some indication of its future value. But before any preservation decision, other than a short-term fix, can be made, a retention decision is vital. Without a clear retention policy a preservation policy can become a haphazard, and even potentially wasteful, exercise. Most material that is accepted in an archive will be retained, although weeding exercises are not unknown, and here too, weeding decisions need to precede preservation decisions. A decision on the format in which material is to be kept also needs to be made.

Material that is acquired for short-term use only is rarely part of a preservation policy, although even in its short life it may well need some conservation treatment. Material of which the intellectual content only is to be retained will be an obvious candidate for surrogating, whether in the form of a microfilm, or in digital format. But although surrogating can be a useful way to preserve the intellectual content of library and archive material, it is not a solution in every case. Frequently the format is as important as, and sometimes even more important than, the information it contains. The physical format alone can provide information over and beyond its content and there are a number of library and archive users who have a real need to consult material in its original format, whether for the study of paper, parchment, ink, or of other writing materials used, or for the study of the composition of the document, or the structure of the book and its binding. Although these are a minority of all library and archive users, their needs should not be forgotten and they are unlikely to wear out the originals. For some purposes of access surrogates can even be preferable to originals, while surrogates, provided they have been made carefully and with suitable equipment, can prolong the life of an original by protecting it from over-handling and repeated copying.

Libraries and archives need to state how surrogates will be used, whether they are catalogued, and whether users will always in the first instance be offered a surrogate in preference to the original. Criteria on which the fate of the originals is based also need to be included. The decision whether or not the original should be retained once a surrogate has been made has been the subject of much debate. Two strong arguments in favour of doing so are that a surrogate will not satisfy all users and, moreover, the surrogate itself may have a limited life-span.

## Storage and access

Long-term retention demands suitable storage conditions and good quality storage equipment, in order to protect the collections and to slow down their physical and chemical deterioration. The nature of the collections themselves, the materials of which they are made, their structure, size and shape, as well as their age, rarity and value, determine the conditions in which they should be stored. Some kinds of material will need greater security, others extra protection, or a different and better-controlled storage environment. Considering the enormous variety of library and archive collections and their often composite nature, there is no such thing as an ideal storage environment suited to everything; compromises have to be made and a balance found. For that reason, the revised British Standard (BS 5454:2000) gives a range of suitable environmental conditions, rather than setting too strict parameters that would neither fit all cases, nor be achievable.

Storage and access are closely linked to security and a preservation policy needs either to include a security policy or be linked to one. This should address the physical security of the building and its perimeter, but also security of access to the collections. Decisions on closed versus open access; conditions of access by staff, contractors, and users to storage areas; security during lending and transport, as well as security of computer systems, including authorized access to and manipulation of data, all have to be considered. The need to safeguard the collections will influence how they are housed. High-security areas can be desirable – even essential – but security that is too strict can defeat itself in case of a sudden emergency. Sensibly controlled access must be a requirement whenever any secure storage is planned. A security policy must include the users; some specialized libraries or archives may wish to limit access to members or users who have been vetted. There might be limitations of access to original material in favour of surrogates. Procedures to be followed in case of a breach of security should also be laid down, and responsibilities for security, both those of the staff and of the users, should be clearly stated.

## Lending, exhibitions and reprographic services

There are a number of other library and archive functions or activities that must be taken into account when a preservation policy is formulated, such as lending, exhibitions and reprographic services. When lending material either for use off the premises or for exhibitions elsewhere, several issues need to be made clear from the start. Reasons for allowing or refusing loans need to be given, including possible restrictions on the loan of certain types of rare or fragile material, or the provision of surrogates instead of originals. Conditions for loan will have to be specified, including those for environmental control, security and handling, while security provisions during transport and during the loan period, as well as responsibility for insurance, need to be determined. Similar considerations apply to exhibitions, whether these are held in the library or archive itself or elsewhere. Restrictions on the type of material that can be exhibited and on the duration of the exhibition; conditions for security, environment and illumination, for the design of the exhibition cases and of furniture or stands; guidelines for support materials and for the handling of objects, need to be clearly set out. Decisions are needed whether material that is lent for exhibition is always first copied. Procedures have to be in place for conservation reports, both before and after the exhibition and for monitoring the material during the exhibition. All these issues have a direct impact on the preservation of the collections.

Likewise, a copying or reprographics policy has to take account of preservation considerations. It needs to include copyright issues, but also to consider frequency of use and frequency of demand for copies. It needs to set out possible restrictions imposed by particular formats, size, or condition of the material to be copied, as well as give guidelines for handling and support. There will have to be rules as to which material may or may not be copied by the users themselves.

## Resources

No preservation policy and no preservation programme, however well and carefully conceived, can be implemented without sufficient funding and without the intelligence, knowledge and energy of people. We can make no assumptions about the provision of resources, and preservation is only one of many library and archive functions that cry out for funding. The balance between acquisition, access, public services, support services and preservation needs careful scrutiny. In different libraries and archives this balance will differ and it is only through seeing the dependencies and relationships of all library and archive activities and functions that a sensible balance can be achieved. Long-term access to both analogue and digital material requires a positive, and in some cases an ongoing, commitment. Neglect is not an option. Developments in technology and in preservation and conservation techniques mean that at least in theory most material can be saved, but time limits apply, especially for electronic formats, and decisions may have to be taken sooner rather than later.

Limited resources demand that we make best use of those we have. This applies to financial resources, but perhaps even more to people. The training and education of staff and users are vital, and so is constant emphasis on awareness-raising throughout an institution and throughout the community. Much more investment is necessary – financial, but equally important, intellectual – in the training of conservators, of preservation managers and of all who handle and use books and documents. Knowledge of historical book structures, of the history of book production and book materials, of past and present conservation techniques and of new technology are all vital if selection for preservation is to be informed and if decisions on treatment are to be intelligent and of long-term benefit to the collections.

## Formulating a preservation policy

When formulating a preservation policy it is useful to begin by stating the rationale for and the scope of the policy. This is followed by a statement of the aims and purposes of the institution and of the purpose and function of the collection. The preservation philosophy follows. Is the emphasis on prevention of damage or on active conservation, on content or on format (or both), on current or future use, on replacement or retention?

Then the needs of the collection should be assessed – looking at its rarity, its intrinsic value, the use that is made of it, the way in which it is stored and its condition – but also at the risks it may be subjected to, both day to day and in case of a disaster. The preservation policy should be linked to acquisition, access and retention; it should either include or refer to policies on collection security, storage and environmental control, and give guidelines for proper handling of the collections, be it for on-site or remote use, for surrogating and for reprographic processes, for exhibitions and loans. It should be supported by accepted and proven standards and by a high level of professional performance.

In order to make sure such a policy is realistic and can be implemented, it must take into account the available resources (financial and human) and, most importantly, it must be a living document: it should be frequently referred to, constantly monitored and regularly updated.

## Preservation strategy and planning

A preservation policy forms the basis for a preservation strategy and for preservation programmes. A preservation strategy which considers how the materials will be preserved, and in what order, needs to be planned like a military campaign, a campaign against damage and decay. First of all we need to define what we want to achieve, what the problems are, how they can be tackled, and in what order. We need to establish what programmes and resources we already have, whether we can use them, and how effective they are. We have to consider the life expectancy, both of the collections and of the buildings that house them, and see whether we make the right and the best use of our buildings. We need to investigate what standards and guidelines exist and how they can be interpreted and applied. We must realize the importance of documentation; we need historical as well as current information about our collections, their past life, their housing and their use, but also about past treatments and treatment decisions, and we must document current actions and treatments. We need to consider the balance between preservation and use, between the original object and a surrogate; and we need to be aware of the significance, meaning and value of the collections. A campaign needs to be funded and a cost–benefit analysis, weighing of short-term cost against long-term benefit, neglect against long-term damage, can support an argument for funding. Proper briefings have to be given to governors and funding bodies, senior management, staff and users, conservators, and all stakeholders and beneficiaries. And a campaign needs leaders: responsibilities will have to be clearly defined and allocated. Then we can draw up our preservation plan and develop our programmes.

In order to tackle our preservation problems in a coherent way (coherent from the point of view of the institution, the collection as a whole and its users), and in order to make best use of our resources, we need to set priorities and we need to be selective. It is neither possible, nor even desirable, to preserve all library and archive material in existence, to look after everything that is produced and received. But our selection needs to be well argued and based on sound criteria. Some criteria can be measured and therefore have a certain objectivity, others cannot be measured and are more subjective. Value, rarity, use, condition and urgency of need are often used as criteria for selection for preservation.

## Value

Value means not only monetary value – a consideration how much an item did cost or how much it would cost to replace it would be but a crude measure. More important are historical or bibliographical value, an estimate of the historical and long-term future value or importance of the content, but also of the value attached to the object or the format. These are difficult to assess, especially when we compare subjects that have no common basis for comparison and when we have to judge future value. Texts that may be important now may well not be so in the future and vice versa. Content value can be judged from different perspectives; we look at literary, cultural, academic or research value, sociological and historical value, as well as at local, national or international value.

Cultural or social value should include all aspects of society, daily life as well as art, music, literature and science, all aspects of the culture of a nation. Academic or research value is not limited to any particular culture or any particular nation. Scholarship is international. Research value needs to be judged not only in the present but also for the future; it is linked with education, with areas for study and subjects of teaching. Sometimes it is difficult to judge whether material is purely of local value or whether it has a wider national or international importance. The origin of the material is often less important than its breadth and depth of content. In all these cases, judgements cannot be made by librarians and archivists alone; the practitioners and users must be involved.

The historical or bibliographical value of a whole collection is often greater than the sum of its parts, while the importance of the individual artefact or object may derive from the information the object itself, its composition, its material, its structure or decoration, or its provenance, can provide; what it can reveal about the economic or social circumstances of its production, about those for whom it was produced and about the culture in which it functioned.

## Rarity

Rarity is something that can be measured. Some material is unique, some has a very low survival rate and is now extremely rare. Some material has value-added characteristics and can be rare or unique because of these. Sometimes material is not rare in itself, but it may be inaccessible. Material may exist somewhere, but for political or geographical reasons not be easily available. Uniqueness or extreme rarity by itself is not, of course, an argument for preservation priority. A judgement also needs to be made about the literary, scientific, historical or cultural importance of the unique document. Nor is it always easy to determine whether something is unique. For much manuscript or archival material it is obvious, but for printed material it is not always easy to know whether something is or is not a duplicate. The rule-of-thumb that nothing produced in the hand-press period is a duplicate must not obscure the fact that some later, machine-produced material can also have specific features that make it unique, and close scrutiny and careful comparison are necessary before a judgement can be made. Moreover, collections, because of the combination of the material, because of the reasons for which or the person by whom they have been put together, can also be unique and would need to be preserved as such.

## Use

Many libraries and archives consider use as one of their most important selection criteria. Both the amount and the kind of use must be considered. Use can be an indication of importance, but the amount of use a collection or an item in a collection gets is not necessarily an absolute. What constitutes high use in one institution may well be considered low use in another. The kind of use that is made of a collection is often more important in determining preservation needs and priority. Material can be used for its content or for its format, or both, it can be used purely for reference or for sustained reading, on and off the premises, it can be used for teaching and for handing round, or it can be used mainly for exhibitions or mainly for copying. Different kinds of usage bring different risks of damage and consequently demand different preservation decisions, some needing to be made more urgently than others. Although use is an important factor in priority setting and selecting for preservation, it should not be the only criterion and lack of use by itself should not be a reason for neglect. A work may be very rarely used, or not used at all at a particular point in time, but it may one day be needed by someone to extend knowledge and deepen understanding.

## Condition of the collection

The physical state of the collection, its condition, must also be taken into account when material is selected for preservation. There are a number of ways in which the condition of a collection can be assessed and a number of models for collection needs assessment have been published (e.g., Eden et al., 1998). Condition is frequently equated with usability – can the material be used without incurring further damage or will it disintegrate?

Before condition can be assessed, the material needs to be examined carefully and knowledgeably. Systematic and non-destructive examination is needed to establish material characteristics, chemical composition, and changes that have taken place or are taking place. This is essential for choosing the right treatments and for setting parameters within which treatment can be carried out safely. A certain amount of knowledge about the historical development and use of library and archive materials, about the kinds of paper, parchment, inks and binding materials that have been used in the past, and their chemical composition, and some knowledge of how these materials have been employed and how they may have changed under the influence of time, usage and different storage environments, all help us to understand why and how the physical and chemical characteristics of the material have changed and why the collection has deteriorated. The physical characteristics and the condition of the material should be carefully documented before starting any treatment, while all materials, chemicals and methods used for treatment should also be recorded.

The degree of damage or deterioration and the speed with which it happens are also important when we are setting priorities for treatment and we need to distinguish between immediate need, when the threat to the survival of the material is acute, and longer-term need, when decay is slow, but may turn critical at some stage. To judge this accurately we need to know the cause of deterioration or the reasons for decay.

However, none of these criteria for selection for preservation and for establishing priority of treatment should be considered in isolation. None by themselves will be sufficient to present a conclusive argument for spending time and money. The balance between and the combination of value, rarity, use, condition and need are important to make sensible selection decisions and to set defensible priorities.

## Costs and monitoring
Planning a preservation programme is only one step, albeit an important one. But before such a programme can be carried out we need to consider what the costs are and what resources will be needed. When planning a preservation programme both direct and indirect costs have to be taken into account. We also need to ensure that the right knowledge and skills

are available or can be made available to carry out the necessary work. Direct costs include labour (staff costs) and materials or consumables, while indirect costs include overheads, both managerial, and building and equipment overheads. Material selected for conservation treatment needs to be fetched and prepared, specifications will have to be written, the material may need to be packed and transported, it may have to be insured if treated away from the library's or archive's own premises, and when it is returned, it needs to be checked, re-shelved, and bills have to be paid. Whether the work is carried out in-house or elsewhere, a conservation workshop will have to be built or found, it will have to be fitted out, insured, maintained and cleaned, equipment will have to be bought or rented and maintained, and light, heating and water need to be provided. Managerial overheads may include computer or other systems to set up and monitor the workflow, to keep count of where the material is at any one time, to keep accounts and to provide the raw information for the necessary management reports.

Any preservation programme needs to be monitored, to ensure that the specifications have been followed, the right treatments have been carried out, and to demonstrate its progress and effectiveness. Both the quantity of the work done – the number of books and documents that have been treated, the amount of time and money that has been spent – and the quality have to be monitored. Quality control is important and the basis for good quality conservation work is a clear and unambiguous specification, drawn up with sufficient knowledge of the material to be conserved, of its needs, but also of the available treatment options and technical possibilities. A dialogue between conservators and curators is essential to come to the right kind of treatment specification, while the right knowledge and skills will then be necessary to ensure that the treatment is carried out as specified with the most suitable materials and in the best possible way. Especially when dealing with external contractors, the specification needs to be detailed and clear. If this cannot be achieved, the quality of the work cannot be monitored.

Records of what has been done and what treatments have been given, which materials and chemicals have been used and what processes have been carried out, are as important as numerical statistics of how many items have been treated and at what cost. All this is needed not only to monitor future behaviour of the treated material and to decide on possible future further treatments, but also to compile management reports that are required by most libraries' and archives' governing bodies. The frequency of reporting and the kinds of report asked for will depend on what the library or archive needs and on what its funding structure is, but keeping careful figures throughout the year will ensure that such reports can be submitted without too much difficulty. Showing what has been achieved over time and at what cost will also help in drawing up new programmes and obtaining funding for them.

## Risk assessment

When considering the needs of library and archive collections in drawing up preservation policies, strategies and programmes, we usually start from a given situation in more or less stable circumstances. However, we need to consider what internal and external threats may be present, what risks our collections and buildings may be facing, both in their normal day-to-day existence and under extreme conditions. An assessment of such threats or risks is an essential basis for preservation planning; it can also be the basis for any plans to prevent, control or manage disasters. Anything that adversely affects a library or archive, its staff, its users, its collections and its services, constitutes a risk and any internal or external threat to the achievement of a library's or archive's objectives needs to be identified and analysed.

Libraries and archives can face a number of risks which prevent them from achieving their objectives, such as the risks of not acquiring material or not being able to make it available, and the risk of losing collections, in their entirety or in part, by accident, through calamities, or through theft, vandalism or terrorism, or through degradation. There are different kinds of risk, different degrees of calamity and the chances that a certain risk will happen and its impact on the library or archive will also differ, depending on the risk itself, on the kind of material in question and on the kind of library or archive concerned. Each library or archive item, each book, document, film, photograph, etc., has its own risk, based on its physical composition, perceived value and purpose.

When conducting a risk assessment we have to start by identifying the risk, for example, the risk of loss or of damage, and then to define its possible cause or causes. Only then can we try to assess what the chances are that such a risk will actually happen, what the degree might be to which it will happen, what the impact or consequences of such a risk will be, what the likely degree or magnitude of that impact is, and when it might happen. This will help us to evaluate the risk. Once we have done that we need to decide how to react. We can decide to bear the risk, the risk itself being quite small, the chances that it will happen not very high, and its likely impact comparatively insignificant. Or we can decide to share it, for instance by insuring against it. We could try to manage the risk, by deciding to reduce or change it, or reduce the likelihood of its happening, or by planning to mitigate its consequences or the likely degree of its impact. Or we could try and avoid the risk altogether by stopping its likely causes or by suspending certain activities that may cause the risk. Obviously, the higher the likelihood and the more serious the impact of a risk, the more likely we are to try to take measures to avoid it. But in order to reduce, change, avoid or stop a risk, we need to know what options we have for doing so. It is useful to list all options and then to evaluate them on their effectiveness, the possibility of implementing them and their possible cost. Then we can choose the option which best suits the circumstances and implement it. However, there may be constraints within which we have to work and the ideal option may sometimes not be possible. Internal constraints (such as lack of staff, lack of skills and knowledge, lack of management support or lack of money) can all hinder the best option from being chosen, as can external constraints (such as political or legal requirements, building restrictions, or historical or artistic considerations). A cost-benefit analysis can help with a risk assessment, identifying not only what the cost and likely benefit of preventing a risk may be, but also what the cost might be of letting it happen. A simple formula for assessing risks would look as follows:

Likelihood/probability + effect/impact → reaction → option → action

## Risk management

Risk management – the prevention of risks and the reaction to them if they could not be prevented – is the basis for disaster management. Prevention is almost always better than cure, provided the consequences are sufficiently dire. Anything that happens unexpectedly and causes heavy damage or loss can be called a disaster. A great deal has been published about disaster management and disaster planning and a brief overview will have to suffice here.

The sensible long-term strategy is to avoid or prevent disasters, or at least to try to mitigate their impact, by careful planning, being prepared, having measures and systems in place to cope. Prevention may require a certain amount of capital investment; it will certainly require time and expertise. Its first step is a full risk assessment, followed by a plan to avoid the serious risks, which need to be prioritized, costed, budgeted for and acted upon. Whatever can be done to prevent risks that are imminent should be done. Some preventive measures will be comparatively simple and inexpensive, others will require more investment, but as there will be long-term benefit, they must be judged on their future economic effectiveness. Preparation will involve raising awareness throughout the institution, allocating responsibilities, training staff, and careful planning for eventualities. Such planning demands surveys of buildings, storage areas and evacuation routes, as well as surveys of collections. Estimates of their relative importance and vulnerability, of their location and their salvation priority will need to be decided and laid down. Contacts will have to be established with security officers, building managers and emergency services. The layout of the building, access to it and to its facilities and equipment need to be clearly mapped. First aid and disaster equipment need to be accessible and external or contract rescue services may need to be on call.

However, disasters cannot always be avoided, and a short-term strategy then needs to be in place. A written emergency or disaster manual, emergency training and practice runs can do much to make a disaster less traumatic and to make those who have to deal with it more confident. When disaster strikes in the form of a fire, a flood, an earthquake or any other sudden and unexpected threat to buildings, staff, users and collections, the first step is to ensure the safety of all people present. Depending on the scale of the disaster, emergency services and the relevant staff need to be contacted. The immediate threat or calamity will have to be stopped, a fire extinguished, main services such as electricity and water supply turned off, and the building made safe, before the damage can be assessed. Further damage has to be guarded against, and damage that has occurred will have to be dealt with. There are several methods for dealing with damaged material, and depending on the type of damage, the types of collection, the kinds of institution and the capabilities of those who carry out the rescue work, the best and most appropriate will have to be chosen. It is as well to remember that there are delaying techniques and not all damaged material will have to be dealt with instantly. Preferably an area will have been identified where damaged collections can be sorted into material that needs to be frozen to arrest decay and to buy time, and material that needs to be cleaned and that can be dried on the premises. Information will have to be provided to senior staff and to users, especially in the cases where services are suspended. Those who actively take part in the rescue work will need to be supported, as working in the aftermath of a disaster is both physically and emotionally exhausting.

Once immediate action has taken place, it is as well to realize that total recovery may take some time. The building or storage areas will have to be repaired, secured, or at least cleaned; the environment will have to be stabilized, damaged collections to be conserved or repaired and to be moved back, and services will have to be restored. Particularly after a fire or a flood, the storage areas and material that has been wet will have to be regularly inspected for possible outbreaks of mould.

Once normal life can be resumed, there is the need to assess what has happened, why, and how it has been dealt with. The success or otherwise of previous planning will have to be judged, lessons learnt, and previous plans may have to be changed. It is in any case good practice to review and, if need be, update any disaster planning to reflect changes in the organization or in its collections and their storage.

## Conclusion

Preservation is integral to a number of core library and archive functions. Consequently, it is imperative to develop a robust preservation policy that provides a clear and coherent blueprint for preservation planning. Once such a policy is in place, preservation activitites such as valuation, access, risk assessment, and disaster planning can be co-ordinated effectively and efficiently, thus maximizing institutional resources and facilitating strategic prevention rather than belated cures.

## Bibliography

The literature concerning all aspects of preservation policy and planning, risk assessment and disaster control is vast. What follows is a highly selective list and does not pretend to be comprehensive.

Anderson, H. and McIntyre, J. E. (1985) *Planning Manual for Disaster Control in Scottish Libraries and Record Offices*, Edinburgh, National Library of Scotland.

Ashley-Smith, J. (1999) *Risk Assessment for Object Conservation*, London, Butterworth and Heinemann.

Baker, N. (2001) *Double Fold: libraries and the assault on paper*, New York, Random House.

Banks, P. and Pilette, R. (eds) (2000) *Preservation Issues and Planning*, Chicago, American Library Association.

Bell, N. and Lindsay, H. (2000) *Benchmarks in Collection Care for UK Libraries*, London, Library and Information Commission.

British Standards Institution (1992) *BS 1153:1992: Recommendations for the processing and storage of silver gelatine type microfilm*, London, BSI.

British Standards Institution (2000a) *BS 5454:2000: Recommendations for the storage and exhibition of archival documents*, London, BSI.

British Standards Institution (2000b) *BS 4971:2000: Repair and allied processes for the conservation of documents*, London, BSI.

Cassar, M. (1993) *Environmental Management: guidelines for museums and galleries*, London, Museums and Galleries Commission.

Cassar, M. (1998) *Cost–Benefit Appraisals for Collection Care: a practical guide*, London, Museums and Galleries Commission.

Cassar, M. and Hutchings, J. (2000) *Relative Humidity and Temperature Pattern Book: a guide to understanding and using data on the museum environment,* London, Museums and Galleries Commission.

de Lusenet, Y. (ed.) (2000) *Preservation Management: between policy and practice,* Amsterdam, European Commission on Preservation and Access.

Eden, P. , Dungworth, N., Bell, N. and Matthews, G. (1998) *A Model for Assessing Preservation Needs in Libraries,* BLRIC Report 125, London, British Library Research and Innovation Centre, British Library.

Edwards, A. and Matthews, G. (2000) *Developing a National Strategy for Preservation Surrogates,* London, Library and Information Commission.

Elkinton, N. E. (ed.) (1992) *Preservation Microfilming Handbook,* Mountain View, CA, Research Libraries Group.

European Commission on Preservation and Access (1997) *Choosing to Preserve: towards a comparative strategy for long-term access to the intellectual heritage,* Amsterdam, European Commission on Preservation and Access.

Feather, J. (1996) *Preservation and the Management of Library Collections,* 2nd edn, London, Library Association Publishing.

Feather, J. and Eden, P. (1997) *National Preservation Policy: policies and practices in archives and record offices,* BLRIC Report 43, London, British Library Research and Innovation Centre, British Library.

Feather, J., Matthews, G. and Eden, P. A. (1996) *Preservation Management: policies and practices in British libraries,* Aldershot, Gower.

Foot, M. M. (1996) Housing our Collections: environment and storage for libraries and archives, *IFLA Journal,* **22**, 110-14.

Foot, M. M. (2001) *Building Blocks for a Preservation Policy,* London, National Preservation Office.

Forde, H. (1991) *The Education of Staff and Users for the Proper Handling and Care of Archival Materials: a RAMP study with guidelines,* Paris, UNESCO.

Forde, H. (1997) Preservation Policies: who needs them?, *Journal of the Society of Archivists,* **18** (2), 165-73.

Fox, L. L. (1996) *Preservation Microfilming: a guide for libraries and archives,* 2nd edn, Chicago, American Library Association.

Gwinn, N. and Wellheiser, J. (2005) *Preparing for the Worst, Planning for the Best: protecting our cultural heritage from disaster,* Munich, Bowker.

Hughes, S. (2001) *Preserving Library and Archive Collections in Historic Buildings*, London, Resource.

International Council on Archives, Committee on Disaster Prevention (1997) *Guidelines on Disaster Prevention and Control in Archives*, Paris, ICA.

International Federation of Library Associations (1998) *Principles for the Care and Handling of Library Materials*, Paris, IFLA Preservation and Conservation Programme.

Kitching, C., Edgar, H. and Milford, I. (2001) *Archival Documents: guide to the interpretation of BS 5454:2000*, London, British Standards Institution.

Matthews, G. and Feather, J. (2003) *Disaster Management for Libraries and Archives*, Aldershot, Ashgate.

McIntyre, J. E. (1998) A Dual Approach to Risk Management, *LIBER Quarterly*, **8**, 448-57.

National Preservation Office (1992a) *Carrying Out a Library Security Survey and Drafting a Security Policy*, London, NPO.

National Preservation Office (1992b) *Microfilms in Libraries: the untapped resource*, London, NPO.

National Preservation Office (1994a) *Security Matters: how to deal with criminal and anti-social behaviour*, London, NPO.

National Preservation Office (1994b) *Preservation: a training manual for library staff*, London, NPO.

National Preservation Office (1996) *Security Matters: designing out crime*, London, NPO.

National Preservation Office (2000a) *Guide to Preservation Microfilming*, London, NPO.

National Preservation Office (2000b) *Good Handling Principles and Practice for Library and Archive Materials*, London, NPO.

National Preservation Office (2000c) *Guidance for Exhibiting Library and Archive Materials*, London, NPO.

National Preservation Office (2003) *Photocopying of Library and Archive Materials*, London, NPO.

National Preservation Office (2005) *Where Shall We Put It? Spotlight on collection storage issues*, London, NPO.

Resource (now: Museums, Libraries and Archives Council) (2002) *Benchmarks in Collection Care for Museums, Archives and Libraries: a self-assessment checklist*, London, Resource.

Resource (now: Museums, Libraries and Archives Council) (2003) *Security in Museums, Archives and Libraries*, 2nd edn, London, Resource.

Sebera, D. (1994) *Isoperms: an environmental management tool*, Washington DC, Commission on Preservation and Access.

Society of Archivists (1996) *Disaster Preparedness: guidelines for archives and libraries*, London, Society of Archivists.

Tanselle, G. (1989) Reproductions and Scholarship, *Studies in Bibliography*, **42**, 25-54.

Tregarthen Jenkin, I. (1987) *Disaster Planning and Preparedness: an outline disaster control plan*, London, British Library.

UNESCO (1998) *Safeguarding the Documentary Heritage: a guide to standards, recommended practices and reference literature related to the preservation of documents of all kinds*, Brussels, Memory of the World Programme.

Wellheiser, J. and Scott, J. (2002) *An Ounce of Prevention: integrated disaster planning for archives, libraries and record centres*, Oxford, Scarecrow Press.

## Some useful websites

CAMiLEON (Creative Archiving at Michigan and Leeds Emulating the Old on the New), www.si.umich.edu/CAMILEON

CoOL (Conservation OnLine), http://palimpsest.stanford.edu

Council on Library and Information Resources (CLIR), Washington DC, www.clir.org

European Commission on Preservation and Access (ECPA), www.knaw.nl/ecpa/

Gateway for Resources and Information on Preservation (GRIP), www.knaw.nl/ecpa/grip

Getty Conservation Institute, http://getty.edu/conservation

International Council on Archives (ICA ), www.ica.org

IFLA (International Federation of Library Associations) Preservation and Conservation (PAC) Programme, www.ifla.org/VI/4/pac.htm

Library of Congress Preservation Office, http://lcweb.loc.gov/preserv

Library Disaster Control Plan (see M25 website), www.M25lib.ac.uk/M25dcp

Museums, Libraries and Archives Council (MLA ), www.mla.gov.uk

National Archives, www.nationalarchives.gov.uk

National Library of Australia, www.nla.gov.au/preserve

National Preservation Office, UK, www.bl.uk/services/preservation

Northeast Document Conservation Center, www.nedcc.org

Research Libraries Group, PRESERV, www.rlg.org/preserv

University College London (UCL), Centre for Sustainable Heritage,
www.ucl.ac.uk/sustainableheritage

UNESCO, www.unesco.org/webworld/index.shtml

# CHAPTER 3

# Intangible heritage: museums and preservation

David Grattan and John Moses

## Introduction

Intangible heritage can have many forms, and the UNESCO Convention on its preservation has made only limited progress so far. The question of whether museums will play a larger role in its preservation is undecided. However, museums already deal with intangible heritage in two main ways. First, museums must consider the inherent intangible aspects of objects, including function or use, religious significance or practice, or artist's intent. Second, museums must consider the preservation of documentation such as written documents, film, photographs, and audio/videotape. This has become particularly important in recent years as the conservation challenges of these ephemeral materials have become more evident. Museums are also increasingly aware of their obligations to aboriginal communities and collections, and must adopt a professional aboriginal approach to the conservation, preservation, and guardianship of tangible and intangible cultural property.

## What is intangible heritage?

Culture is not only demonstrated through tangible artefacts but is also manifested through intangible forms, such as language, music, theatre, attitudes, gestures, practices, customs and a whole range of other forms. Intangible heritage includes voices, values, traditions, languages, oral history, folk life, creativity, adaptability and indeed all that is distinctive of a people (International Council of Museums, 2004). This distinctiveness is popularly perceived through cuisine, clothing, forms of shelter, traditional skills and technologies, religious ceremonies, manners, customs, performing arts, storytelling and so forth. Many believe that globalization is a threat to intangible heritage (Galla, 2004), hence there is wide recognition that this form of heritage needs to be safeguarded. Accordingly, in 1993 UNESCO developed a Convention for this purpose. As of March 2006, 31 of the 191 member states of UNESCO have either approved or ratified the Convention.

However, concerns about intangible heritage are widespread and even though many nations are unable to sign, there are in fact many initiatives and much discussion about the topic. This theme was the topic of an International Council of Museums (ICOM) meeting in Seoul, in October 2004, and this was entirely appropriate as South Korea, a country with a very rich heritage, is one of the signatory nations.

Regardless of whether or not member states ratify the Convention, most are already concerned with preservation of intangible heritage in one way or another. It is open to question whether organizations such as museums or archives will have primary responsibility for safeguarding intangible heritage. It became clear at the ICOM meeting in South Korea that it is not a given that states will use museums as their primary instruments for the protection of intangible heritage, and it could easily be envisioned that Ministries of Culture or Heritage, or religious organizations could assume major responsibilities.

What is certain, however, is that museums and archives have for a long time maintained a great interest in intangible heritage. This is because it is simply not possible to separate museum collections from living cultures and it is equally impossible when considering any artefact to dissociate the intangible from the tangible. In fact, the intangible attributes of objects make them worthy of preservation.

A UNESCO position paper (2004) examined the role of museums in intangible heritage preservation and concluded that when considering the traditional roles of the museum - acquiring, conserving, researching, communicating and exhibiting - the only two that were problematic for museums were acquiring and conserving. It was suggested that these notions might '(arguably) contribute to fossilizing it' (UNESCO, 2004, 2; Nas, 2002). This seems an extreme stance.

Perhaps a more useful approach towards the preservation of the intangible was that advanced by Lyndel V. Prott (1999), who pointed out that intangible heritage is exceedingly complex, and that each aspect needs to have an appropriate method of safeguarding suited to its needs. In other words, instead of asking whether museums are the right organizations, Prott's more pragmatic approach looks at needs first, and is very useful as a starting point. What he did was to take a number of classes of intangible heritage (such as language, oral history, traditional religion and belief, sacred images and themes, etc.), consider the objective, then the needs, and finally the means of safeguarding each, as shown in Example 2.1.

## Example 2.1
### Prott's approach to preservation of the intangible

*Objective:* to preserve threatened languages.

*Needs:* to maintain a viable language community, a minimum number of mother-tongue speakers.

*Means:* endangered-language programmes; mother-tongue or bilingual education programmes; recording of elderly speakers; 'living cultural treasures' programme for epic and poetry reciters; prize for oral cultural heritage.

For this activity – and most of the others Prott presented – it is clear that the museum, as traditionally understood, is obviously not the appropriate organization for safeguarding, although it can play a part. However, newly developing cultural centres within aboriginal or traditional communities do combine many of these functions and also preserve, research and display collections.

## Traditional role of the museum

Despite the above limitations, museums have and have always had a role in preserving intangible heritage. All objects have intangible aspects, and it is these that make objects engage our attention. For example, if we see a pen in an exhibit, it is just a pen. However, if we are told that it was the actual pen Thomas

Hardy used to write *Tess of the d'Urbervilles*, then it becomes an object of interest and fascination. A pen is just a static object and in reality it is the novels that are interesting rather than the pen used to write them, but there are many other objects in museums in which the function is more significant than the material qualities of the object: musical instruments are good examples. If the intangible is to be safeguarded, is it enough just to preserve the material appearance of the object? A musical instrument must be played. Beyond that, people must have the skills to play it well, there must be music to play, there must be an audience to enjoy it, to sing to it, to dance to it, etc. For the intangible heritage to be truly safeguarded all this must happen.

The relevance of the intangible qualities of objects lies at the heart of the ongoing debate about use versus preservation. If the material essence of an object is prized above all else, then usage that has the potential of wear and increased risk of loss or damage must be avoided at all cost. If, however, it is appreciated that the intangible aspects are in fact more important than the material, then we appreciate that it is the *ability to use the object*, and not the actual object itself, that must be preserved. It is increasingly being appreciated by conservators that their role is to facilitate this use rather than to protect the material qualities of the object. What value is a book if it cannot be read, or a painting that cannot be seen? How can we appreciate a steam engine that must forever be stationary, or an aircraft that must remain earthbound? For objects to be preserved, they must engage the user in some way, they must have a constituency among the public that cares about their survival. Thus the purpose of conservation is in transition as it becomes more focused on allowing objects to recapture some of their original function.

## Documentation

The principal role for museums and archives in safeguarding intangible heritage is in collecting, managing and preserving documentation, that is, documentation of intangible heritage, such as language or traditions, but also of the attributes, history and creation of objects in the collection. In Lyndel Prott's article (1999), recording was mentioned in nearly every category as one of the key elements in the means of preservation. Koch (1999) has pointed out that 'audiovisual archives hold unique materials that document the world's intangible cultural heritage', and she gave specific examples. While some see preservation or documentation as activities which might contribute to the fossilization of the living intangible heritage, it is very clear, however, that recording plays an integral role in the preservation of intangible heritage.

Accompanying this rediscovery of the importance of intangible qualities of objects is a growing concern about preserving such characteristics. Again this means that the documentation surrounding the object is of importance. It is perhaps easiest to understand how documentation of intangible elements relates to artefacts in the domain of art. A major consideration of any paintings curator or art conservator is to understand the intent of the artist. Intent is not always totally evident on examination of the work of any given artist. However, in order to exhibit or store or treat works, it becomes vital to know what the artist was trying to accomplish and how he or she produced the work. This information is often recorded in interviews with artists, and naturally conventional audiotape, videotape and other modern means are employed to record this.

However, once the requirement to develop and preserve documentation is established, then the material aspects of the documentation become the concern of conservation specialists. In a material sense this could consist of photographs, videotape, audiotape, paper records including notes, sketch books, etc. It could also include more material investigations of the artist's materials, techniques and tools.

Documentation can take many physical forms – it can be a written account, or a photographic record – but increasingly it has taken on the material form of magnetic media as audio or videotape. Latterly, these technologies are giving way to the use of optical media such as DVDs or CD-ROMs. And herein lies a major preservation problem for museums and archives, because magnetic media have extremely poor preservation characteristics and there are many uncertainties surrounding optical media.

Magnetic tape has a short life-span of about 20 years before the actual information becomes distorted and increasingly unreadable. The material properties of the tape itself are not long-lasting. In a magnetic tape, the usual construction method is to embed the very finely divided powder of a magnetic metallic oxide within a polyester urethane copolymer adhesive binder. This forms the magnetic layer in which the recorded information is contained. Unfortunately, the adhesive binder breaks down by a process which is accelerated by atmospheric moisture and heat. It is termed a hydrolytic process and is similar to the way in which acetate film or paper breaks down. It is inevitable and unstoppable, and exhibits itself as 'sticky shed', in which the binder actually becomes detached from the tape.

A fundamental problem of all non-traditional media is that they cannot be read without the use of equipment. Unfortunately, technology is constantly evolving, and access to obsolete systems depends on the preservation of devices capable of reading the information. While the public is familiar with changes such as the displacement of eight-track tape and reel-to-reel systems with audio cassette tapes, and the almost total success of VHS tapes in comparison with the Beta system, the situation is much more complex than might be generally appreciated. For example, there are currently at least 15 formats of analogue videotape and, according to one source, there have been approximately 65 NTSC (Never Twice the Same Colour: the US format for broadcast television) formats since 1956, and many more have come and gone in the last 50 years. It would be very difficult for any institution to maintain such a variety of recording equipment in serviceable condition, although many larger organizations do attempt this. We are now seeing the replacement of these with digital optical formats such as CD-ROMs and DVDs. There are questions as to how much longer equipment that will read the multifarious forms of videotape and audiotape will remain available. We are also aware that use of CD-ROMs and DVDs is finite.

Thus electronic recording techniques of all kinds are both a threat and an aid to the preservation of intangible heritage. A greater awareness of their limitations needs to be communicated.

## Aboriginal communities and collections

A major trend throughout the world, and especially in North America, is the repatriation of cultural heritage to communities. We are moving into what Ruth Phillips (2005) has termed the 'Second Museum Age'. Intrinsic in this trend is the dispersal (or, to choose a better word, re-placement) of parts of existing collections to the communities that created them. Where this issue is perhaps most sharply drawn is within the relationship of museums to aboriginal societies. It is wrong to generalize, and certainly as a Canadian I can only speak of North American aboriginal societies. However, I will make the following generalizations as initial premises.

An almost universal aboriginal approach to material objects is to value the intangible aspects as having much more worth than the tangible. This arises from a more holistic approach to preservation, where the concern is dominated by the need to preserve a full range of cultural elements, including language, dance, ceremony and religious values. Partly this is because the survival of aboriginal society is more threatened, but it is also because of a traditional way of thinking, which has been eloquently expressed by Viviane Gray, a Mi'gmaq from the Listuguj First Nation in Quebec, Canada. She stated that in her tradition, 'every created object is sacred whether it is old or new and should be treated with respect. In the case of older objects or those of our ancestors, they usually have songs and/or dances associated with their care and they always have a story' (Gray, 2001, 8-9). It is clear that many of the same issues arise in broader society, except that within the aboriginal communities they are more starkly drawn. However, because of that, the broader community can perhaps learn that material aspects are overvalued.

As conservator and Six Nations band member John Moses has observed, the intangible means more than merely the abstract or the theoretical, and we limit our thinking when we restrict our conception of the intangible properties of culture solely to the immaterial. Conservators of ethnographic artefacts, particularly those who are of indigenous heritage themselves, can provide an intellectual bridge in linking the goals of the mainstream conservation profession to the cultural preservation aspirations of traditional aboriginal communities and indigenous populations enclaved within contemporary nations and states.

For perhaps a majority of aboriginal communities in Canada today, language retention and language revitalization - as a function of the legacy of the residential school experience in this country - are *the* main cultural heritage priorities. The aboriginal imperative remains the perpetuation of all aspects of any given culture, and not just that which happens to be captured within three-dimensional material objects.

Speaking specifically of Indian peoples in Canada (as among the distinct Indian, Inuit and Metis populations which together constitute the legally defined 'aboriginal peoples of Canada'), it can be said that the majority base their traditional method of social organization upon certain customary law traditions which share common features. These customary laws:

- are imparted orally
- emphasize group rights and property held in common over private property and individual rights
- typically emphasize the importance of communally held properties, often originally granted by cultural heroes or semi-mythic personalities to specific clans or lineages, as the tangible proofs of continuing rights of access to lands and other resources.

This aboriginal emphasis on group rights and property held in common, then, is what makes these indigenous law systems most obviously distinct from western or Euro/North American legal regimes, which are codified in text, and wherein protections concerning private property and individual rights are paramount.

Thus objects do not exist in a vacuum, but are parts of different elaborate complexes which will include associated songs, dances, oratory and other kinds of performance. Physical objects are not complete in themselves, but only make sense within the originating culture when they can still be associated with the correct body of ritual. These bodies of ritual, then, are what constitute the intangible heritage encoded within any given object. Our primary challenge as conservators within this paradigm rests in ensuring the continued integrity of the physical attributes of material culture, so that the embedded intangible attributes of that cultural property are also preserved. This is not as obtuse as it sounds, and we can meet these challenges in a concrete way by integrating features of traditional care into routine museum collection care and exhibitions practices; and making a great effort to train more aboriginal conservators in mainstream methods while incorporating aspects of traditional indigenous knowledge into mainstream conservation practice.

## The nature of the preservation problem: how to cope with modern media

Many archives, libraries, museums and cultural centres have collected large quantities of information in formats such as videotapes and audiotapes. As technology advances, they are also making increased use of DVDs and CD-ROMs as storage media. Cultural centres are smaller institutions and, unlike larger organizations, have little or no in-house capacity for conservation. Furthermore, the serious problems of conservation posed by such media are only just being addressed by major national institutions, and the techniques employed and the budgets are quite beyond the scope of aboriginal cultural centres.

One way to reduce losses is to transfer the recording from old tape to new tape: a process called migration. The difficulty is, however, that with each migration there are data losses. After the process has been repeated four or five times, the original is likely to be reduced to mush. Once the videotape or audiotape data has been transferred to digital format, however, the losses during a migration become less of a problem. Furthermore, the lifetime of a CD-ROM is likely to be four times that of a magnetic tape-based recording. However, at present, digitization of video is a risk as DVDs and CD-ROMs do not have the storage capacity to hold all the information contained in a standard two-hour VHS videotape. Hence, for storage on DVD, video data requires compression, and thus there is always a risk of loss of quality. If digitization is the only option available, then DVDs and CD-ROMs do need to be considered. However, the current advice is to make sure that tapes are being stored in as good a condition as possible and to test carefully before adopting a given digitization service. One other issue should be considered: deterioration may be gradual, but loss is catastrophic rather than gradual, that is, it happens suddenly and without warning.

There are many commercial organizations that will convert video to DVD format; the cost varies from between £7 sterling and £30 for a two-hour videotape. Current information suggests that the longevity of the DVD/CD-ROM medium will probably be from 50 to 100 years. Initial results from research at the Canadian Conservation Institute (CCI) suggest that these values might be optimistic. However, it is unlikely that current DVD technology will endure that long before being replaced by another commercial format. Because of this and because of the compression issue there are some who argue that the DVD/CD-ROM is not a preservation solution and that hard drives can be used to store uncompressed video data, but this is an expensive approach.

## What are the practical responses to the problems of documentation?

Because it is less of a technical challenge and because CD-ROM technology is easily affordable and accessible, some museum organizations have pioneered their own 'digitization as preservation' projects. The Canadian Conservation Institute/Northwest Territories Archives Fort Rae Pilot Project, described below, was directly aimed at preserving the intangible heritage of aboriginal communities in north Canada.

Excellent equipment and high-quality recording media are now far more affordable than was the case for professional analogue recording less than a decade ago. Norm Glowach and John Poirier of NWT Archives, with Tom Strang of CCI developed a partnership to disseminate this new technology. CCI had been considering the development of a portable computer workstation for migration of audio recordings. The NWT Archives had been thinking along similar lines, and had considerable experience with outreach in small communities, as well as the technical expertise to train users and maintain systems. Tom Strang and Norm Glowach designed and assembled a portable Macintosh system based on Digidesign Protools equipment. This was packed in a custom-built shipping case and delivered to Yellowknife in the far north of Canada where, after a final check, some improvements were made. According to Glowach and Poirier (2003, 157–8):

> There is some urgency. Residential schools as well as other forces for assimilation have seriously affected use of aboriginal languages in the North. Only a few people speak some languages. Other languages are much healthier. In general, though, the most accomplished speakers are elderly. Transmission of languages to later generations is not occurring at a rate that bodes well for the continued health of the languages. As a result, much of the classical vocabulary and

grammar of these languages exist only on sound recordings. Many of these sound recordings are of people who have passed away. Many recordings are held in small communities under poor storage conditions without proper organization or a preservation plan. Important materials have been lost due to arson and poor management.

While construction took place, Territorial Archivist Richard Valpy made arrangements with the Dogrib Traditional Knowledge Project in the community of Fort Rae (a one-hour drive north of Yellowknife) to test the equipment. The NWT Archives had previously worked closely with this group in providing advice on the organization and preservation of its work, developing a solid framework for the pilot project.

The system was delivered to Fort Rae in May 2001, whereupon Norm Glowach trained staff in its use. Those being trained had some computer skills but no experience in sound recording. The preservation project continued to operate until late 2002. The equipment operated very reliably, and one staff member became very adept in operating the system. There is not yet a final count of the number of items digitized, but the quality of digitized product was very good. Glowach and Poirier noted that, just as for videotape, commercial digitization services can be used, but this may well not be cost-effective for archives or community centres in remote locations or with large collections.

Ultimately, the most effective means of preservation is to achieve a society which can perpetuate its values, techniques, traditions and language. However, at present, we are all subject to an unprecedented onslaught of pop culture and materialistic values, so this is a major challenge. Non-traditional techniques, such as video recording, may well be necessary to safeguard the knowledge of traditional ways of life, to preserve and document stories, to underpin the use of threatened languages and to perpetuate ceremonial traditions.

## References

Galla, A. (2004) Museums and Intangible Heritage, *ARTery*, Special Issue and co-publication of *ARTeFACT*, **9** (1), 11–13, http://rspas.anu.edu.au/papers/heritage/museums_%20Intangible_Heritage_ARTery.pdf.

Glowach, N. and Poirier, J. (2003) Computer-based Sound Recording Preservation and its Application in Small Communities. In *Preservation of Electronic Records: new knowledge and decision making, postprints of symposium 2003 15-18 September,* Ottawa, Canadian Conservation Institute, 157-164.

Gray, V. (2001) The Importance of the Object (II), *ICOM Canada Bulletin,* **13** (June), www.rcip.gc.ca/Resources/Icom/English/e_jun_01.html#importance.

International Council of Museums (2004) Introductory Literature, *20th ICOM Conference: Museums and Intangible Heritage,* ICOM 2-8 October, http://icom.museum/general-conference2004.html.

Koch, G. (1999) Cultural Conservation: a two-way consultation. In *Safeguarding Traditional Cultures: a global assessment of the 1989 UNESCO Recommendation on the Safeguarding of Traditional Culture and Folklore,* Washington DC, Center for Folklife and Cultural Heritage, Smithsonian Institution, www.folklife.si.edu/resources/Unesco/koch.htm.

Nas, P. J. (2002) Masterpieces of Oral and Intangible Culture: reflections on the UNESCO World Heritage list, *Current Anthropology,* **43** (1), 139-48.

Phillips, R. B. (2005) Re-placing Objects: historical practices for the second museum age, *Canadian Historical Review,* **86** (1), 83-110.

Prott, L. V. (1999) Some Considerations on the Protection of the Intangible Heritage: claims and remedies. In *Safeguarding Traditional Cultures: a global assessment of the 1989 UNESCO Recommendation on the Safeguarding of Traditional Culture and Folklore,* Washington DC, Center for Folklife and Cultural Heritage, Smithsonian Institution, www.folklife.si.edu/resources/Unesco/prott.htm.

UNESCO (1993) *Convention for the Safeguarding of the Intangible Cultural Heritage,* http://portal.unesco.org/culture/en/ev.php-URL_ID=16429&URL_ DO=DO_TOPIC&URL_SECTION=201.html.

UNESCO (2004) *The Roles of Museums in Safeguarding Intangible Cultural Heritage,* UNESCO Convention, October, position paper for the expert meeting 5-7 April 2004, http://portal.unesco.org/culture/es/file_download.php/ c9447d7eefbc4806acf8c0fb880409b3Position+Paper+-++ Museums+and+Living+Cultural+Heritage.pdf.

# CHAPTER 4

# Surrogacy and the artefact

## Marilyn Deegan

### Introduction

This chapter deals with the relationship between an artefact and different kinds of surrogate representation of that artefact in the digital world. It discusses the difficult problem of the authenticity and authentication of digital data, and some of the technical methods of authenticating data. The use of digital data as a preservation alternative is also dealt with.

With the advent of photographic techniques for copying documents, conservation of the originals became easier. Documents could be, and were, reproduced as facsimiles in books or on microfilm and these were offered to the readers as a substitute for the originals, thus preserving the originals from further damage. The documentary heritage has always been at risk of damage or destruction through natural or human forces: fire, flood, warfare or neglect. In the last 150 years, a new danger has threatened: the '"slow fires" of acidic paper' (Kenney, 1997, 2), which has necessitated the large-scale microfilming of millions of pages of documents over many decades in order that the content is not lost. Many digital reformatting initiatives grew out of earlier microfilming projects, lighting the '"fast fires" of digital obsolescence' (Kenney, 1997, 2).

Substitution of originals with other objects that simulate their content does, of course, pose its own problems: when is a facsimile a satisfactory surrogate for the object itself? This depends on both the needs of the reader and the quality of the reproduction, and is not an easy question to answer. The relationship between any original object and a reproduction of it is problematic, and is a question which has exercised theorists and practitioners of artefactual disciplines for many years. In his seminal essay 'The Work of Art in an Age of Mechanical Reproduction', Walter Benjamin states that: 'Even the most perfect reproduction ... is lacking in one element: its presence in time and space. ... This unique existence of the work ... determined the history to which it was subject throughout its time of existence.' (Benjamin, 1973 (reprinted 1992), 214).

The authenticity of surrogates and their acceptability to readers is of major concern, but so too is the preservation and conservation of these surrogates themselves. One great advantage of mechanically produced surrogates is the possibility of preservation through multiplication of the numbers of copies. In the analogue world, this itself results in some degradation through re-copying; in the digital world, every copy is theoretically an exact copy of its precursor, even after many generations of copying. The crucial questions to ask in the debate about the preservation of originals by the use of surrogates is: what is it that we are preserving and for whom? Are we preserving the objects themselves or the information that they contain? With certain unique, intrinsically valuable and highly significant works – the Book of Kells, the Beowulf manuscript – the object itself is as important as what it says. With more ephemeral materials, such as newspapers or government documents, there may be key issues or volumes where it is worth preserving the originals. However, in general it is probably the content, and the physical arrangement of that content, that needs to be preserved, rather than the objects themselves. These are matters of much controversy, as we will see below.

## Authenticity of digital data

Authenticity of digital documents must be distinguished from authentication as generally defined in the digital world. MacKenzie defines 'authenticity' of a documentary source as 'reliability over time' (2000, 59) while 'authentication' is a term usually used for the process of validating who is allowed access to digital data, and what they might be permitted to do with it. As Rothenberg (2000, 1) has pointed out, 'whenever informational entities are used, and for whatever purpose, their suitability relies on their authenticity'. He goes on to remark that 'the technological issues surrounding the preservation of digital information entities interact with authenticity in novel and profound ways'. This is a key and crucial issue in the preservation of digital data, as validating its authenticity is so much more problematic than in the analogue world. It is frighteningly easy to change a digital document, leaving no trace, no ghostly palimpsest to tell us what was there before. If we alter the words on a written document, generally we can decipher the original and the changes become part of the cultural accretion of meaning gained by the document. A digital document always appears pristine – despite changes made by accident or design – and this means that if two readers are discussing a work, they may not always know that they are using the same version, or if there has been some hidden change. One major consequence of this is that digital data may not be legally valid, and an analogue version may need to be stored for legislative purposes. In order that digital data can be considered legally valid, certain conditions need to be met.

As Cullen (2000, 3) says, 'the problems of preserving digital objects have received more attention than questions of authentication. ... But why preserve what is not authentic?' Users of libraries and archives have, in the past, relied on curators to validate the authenticity of the resources on offer. Curators are trained to know what they have and what its status is, and they rely on a broad professional network in the production and care of the documentary heritage. They purchase materials from reputable sources, have access to experts who can be called upon for second opinions, and they have bodies of meta-information (catalogues, bibliographies, etc.) regarding the provenance and history of rarer works. Forgery or misidentification is not unknown, but the former is a painstaking and difficult process. There are also physical characteristics of originals which can reveal information about the age, provenance or history of an object. And falsification is actually much more difficult than creating the object in the first place. There is a wonderful example of this in the Kipling short story 'Dayspring Mishandled', written in 1928. A character forges a 15th century copy of a supposedly lost work by Chaucer, found bound into the covers of an old Bible. The forger has to create 15th century inks, purchase vellum from the period and even grind his own flour with a millstone to make paste, as well as composing the 'lost' poetry fragment in the first place. How much easier this is in the age of digital data. As

Bearman and Trant (1998, 3) point out of forgery in the digital world, 'the underlying technology makes purposeful fakery easier and more tempting'.

## How to authenticate digital documents

Digital authentication is difficult, and it is a problem which will increase over time as digital documents are preserved for the long term. Security of digital archives is, of course, of paramount importance, but it is not a topic that we propose to tackle here. Version control is also problematic, as very slightly different digital versions of the same exemplar could be circulating without being discovered, unless the changes are fully documented throughout the life of the resource. Digital dissemination is almost unthinkably rapid, as people who have circulated a private e-mail to a public discussion list have sometimes found to their embarrassment.

Some accepted system of authenticity validation needs to exist in the digital world, but this is difficult to establish and to enforce for all potential uses and purposes. Markers which can be tracked can be added to the digital object (watermarks, digital signatures), but hackers are never very far behind such developments, and they can be expensive to maintain. Responsible agencies producing digital documents are likely to use metadata structures, collection records, or unique document identifiers which can be checked, but again these could be subject to abuse. Librarians and archivists are going to have to face questions of digital authenticity more often than they faced the same issues in the analogue world, and the solutions are likely to be more diverse.

In order that digital data can be considered legally valid, certain conditions need to be met. There are now legal recommendations that must be followed if digital documents are to be considered authentic in the eyes of the law, and, for example, admissible as evidence in court (see British Standards Institution, 2004; Digital Forensics Center, n.d.). Legal implications will also need to be considered when planning long-term archiving. What is key in this situation is creating audit trails to record the life-cycle of the digital object: for instance, who is responsible for it, how it is stored, and who is allowed access to it. Validating of individual documents can also be done using 'digital signatures'. Digital signatures are created and verified by cryptography, using what is known as 'public key cryptography'. This employs an algorithm using two different but mathematically related 'keys': one for creating a digital signature or transforming data into a seemingly unintelligible form, and another key for verifying a digital signature or returning the message to its original form (see American Bar Association, n.d.). In a library, the requirements are not likely to concern legal issues, but validating authenticity is nonetheless important. As Bearman and Trant (1998, 8) state, 'to determine which methods are suited for what purpose, it is critical that we better understand the functional requirements for authenticity on the part of creators and potential users of digital resources'. In 2000, the Research Libraries Group (RLG) and OCLC (Online Computer Library Center) began to work on the notion of 'trusted digital repositories' for research organizations. A working group was created to reach consensus on the characteristics and responsibilities of trusted digital repositories for large-scale, heterogeneous collections held by cultural organizations. A major report was produced (RLG-OCLC, 2002) which has been highly influential in the digital archiving community.

## Surrogate versus original

Can surrogates ever truly replace or faithfully represent the original? There is a rather extreme example of features in an original which would be impossible to preserve (at least with any current technologies) in *The Social Life of Information* (Brown and Duguid, 2000, 173-4). One of the authors reports an experience when researching in an archive of 19th-century letters in the USA. Dust from the letters was causing him to have allergic reactions; he covered his nose with a handkerchief and continued working, wishing that someone had digitized the letters so that he could read them on a clean computer screen. He became aware that the person next to him was behaving very oddly: he would pick up each letter in his box, scrutinize it and then slowly sniff it all over. Unable to work out the reason for this strange behaviour, the author finally asked his neighbour what he was doing. He replied that he was a medical historian and was trying to detect traces of vinegar which was sprinkled on letters in cholera outbreaks, as he felt that he might be able to correlate the journeys of the letters with the spread of the cholera. For this scholar, there could be no substitute for the physical object.

The notion of representation of an original by a surrogate is always problematic and in some sense it is always a falsification. For instance, photographs of buildings or sculptures and transcriptions or editions of texts are interpretations as much as they are representations. Creating surrogates can never replicate or preserve everything about an original object, but creating no surrogates could mean that everything is lost in the case of fragile or compromised originals: brittle books printed on acid-based paper, older newspapers, ancient and medieval books and manuscripts, crumbling sculptures, ruined buildings, photographs on glass plates and explosive nitrate film stock.

## Disposal of originals and their replacement by surrogates

We discussed briefly above the advisability or otherwise of replacing originals with surrogates. The most controversial questions here arise when the actual disposal of the originals is proposed. Sometimes there is no real choice to be made. For instance, the Department of Preservation and Collection Maintenance at Cornell University Library (2004a) recommends that for brittle books, a printed photocopy surrogate is created on archival paper, and the original then discarded. This is done using a digital scanning process, and therefore digital images are also produced. The Cornell Brittle Books Project also experimented with Computer Output to Microform technologies to create preservation microfilm copies of the books. The content is therefore safe for the long term. Cornell has become a world leader in digital reformatting and preservation, and runs many courses and workshops on the topic (Cornell University Library, 2004b).

The decision to discard originals by libraries and archives is never taken lightly, but over time materials do have to be discarded for reasons of space and cost. This is not a new issue: repositories have always discarded materials to make way for new items. In the past, materials were sometimes reused. Vellum, for instance, was so costly that it was scraped down and reused, which has paradoxically allowed the recovery of materials that were not actually supposed to survive. The Digital Image Archive of Medieval

Music (DIAMM), for example, has recovered music from 15th-century fragments of vellum that had been used for other purposes, such as binding reinforcements for non-musical sources. Vellum is so durable that it was possible to recover readings, despite damage by water, dirt, rats, glue or the effects of being stuck down to a wooden board for 600 years or more, and some hitherto unknown pieces of medieval music have been discovered in this way (Craig-McFeely and Deegan, 2005).

If some economical means of preserving access to the content can be found, this is often done. This process is part of the responsible stewardship of cultural materials by librarians and archivists, but there are times when these issues become matters of public concern. In 2000, for instance, there was mounting controversy in Britain and the USA about the jettisoning by major libraries of some of their historic newspaper collections. These collections were all preserved on microfilm, but the disposal of originals caused an outcry in the press. Major libraries, such as the Library of Congress and the British Library, have been microfilming newspapers for many decades in order to preserve the historical record rather than the objects, but the critics of the disposal policy advanced many arguments for the retention of the paper copies. As a society, we are wedded to objects rather than surrogates – even if this causes expensive problems – and some of the objections to the disposal were romantic rather than rational.

The main protagonist in this debate was the American novelist Nicholson Baker, who wrote an impassioned article in the *New Yorker* in July 2000. Baker accuses the major public libraries of a massive deception about the state of historic newspaper collections: he suggests that their claims that these newspapers are deteriorating so fast as to be almost beyond preservation are not true, and that they have been microfilming these collections for cynical reasons. 'Librarians have misled us: for more than 50 years, they have disparaged paper's residual strength, while remaining as "blind as lovers" (as Allen Veaner, former editor of *Microform Review*, once wrote) to the failings and infirmities of film' (Baker, 2000, 55; see also Baker, 2001). It is not the microfilming that is so objectionable to Baker, but the disposal of the originals.

As Cox (2000) points out in his critique of Baker's piece, 'there are never any easy answers [in the preservation of information] and, at best, solutions may bring as many additional problems with them as what they are supposedly resolving'. In a debate about this matter in the *Times Literary Supplement*, Pearson (2000) remarks that 'critics are happy to ignore the realities of choice over the use of resources which any major library must face', and he goes on to suggest that large-scale digitization programmes might provide the answer. While this would not solve the original versus surrogate debate, the presentation of newspapers in digital form – especially if this is enhanced by indexing (preferably using indexes generated automatically) – provides greatly improved access and, with good digital archiving, could preserve them for the long term. If there are still issues around the preservation of digital surrogates, then microfilm can be retained as the preservation copy.

## Digital surrogacy: is it a preservation alternative?

The example given above of the microfilming and possible destruction of newspapers begs the question: could digital surrogacy replace tried and tested analogue methods? Is digital preservation well enough understood and sufficiently robust for it to replace photographic techniques? Microfilm is predicted to last 500 years; other photographic materials, especially colour film, are perhaps less durable, but they have been in existence for long enough for there to be some knowledge of deterioration rates. The costs of storage are known and can be predicted into the future, and the surrogates generally do not require costly and time-consuming processes to be carried out on them every few years, as is the case with digital objects. Many librarians and archivists are still cautious about the digital medium as a preservation alternative, feeling that there has not been enough research into the long-term issues – and, in particular, costs – around the archiving of digital information for indefinite periods. Few librarians would de-accession originals and put all their trust in digital storage without perhaps having also a film surrogate as an insurance policy.

Another issue that must be addressed is the common view that digitization should only ever happen once, and then the digital image be preserved for posterity. Careful analysis of the relative costs of storing digital and analogue surrogates may, in some cases, reveal that it could be more cost-effective to rescan originals than to store archive-quality digital files. The determining factor may be the age and condition of the original itself: if digitization is undertaken as a rescue strategy, then it is probably advisable to produce archive-quality files and accept the attendant costs. If, however, it is carried out to provide access to images from media that are in good condition and are relatively stable, then capturing access-quality files and rescanning later if needed could prove to be more cost-effective. Harvard University calculated the costs of scanning and storing digital images from 1,800 5 × 4 transparencies. At $5 per scan, the total cost of scanning is $9,000. To archive the master digital images costs $1,900 per year, and to store the photographic originals costs $3.55. It would therefore be cheaper to rescan later if the images are needed for more than five years (Chapman, personal communication).

## Conclusion

The relationship between an artefact and its various surrogates is a problematic one, and has to be carefully thought through in all aspects of preservation management. In the digital world, the authenticity and authentication of a mass of seemingly identical copies of an original can cause great confusion, but increasingly there are means of validating and tracking surrogates. Preservation managers, whether dealing with analogue or digital surrogates, need to be keenly aware of these issues.

Note: Some of the material presented here first appeared in Chapter 8, 'Preservation', of Deegan and Tanner (2002).

## References

American Bar Association (n.d.) *Digital Signature Guidelines*,
    www.abanet.org/scitech/ec/isc/dsg-tutorial.html.
Baker, N. (2000) Deadline: the author's desperate bid to save America's past,
    *The New Yorker*, (24 July), 42–61.
Baker, N. (2001) *Double Fold: libraries and the assault on paper*, New York,
    Random House.
Bearman, D. and Trant, J. (1998) Authenticity of Digital Resources: towards a
    statement of requirements in the research process, *D-Lib Magazine*,
    (June), 1–12, www.dlib.org/dlib/june98/06bearman.html.

Benjamin, W. (1973, reprinted 1992) The Work of Art in an Age of Mechanical Reproduction. In *Illuminations*, London, Fontana Press.

British Standards Institution (2004) *Code of Practice for Legal Admissibility and Evidential Weight of Information Stored Electronically*, Standard Number BIP 0008-1:2004, London, BSI, www.bsonline.bsi-global.com/search/item/977717.

Brown, J. S. and Duguid, P. (2000) *The Social Life of Information*, Boston, MA, Harvard Business School Press.

Cornell University Library (2004a) *Brittle Books*, www.library.cornell.edu/preservation/index.html.

Cornell University Library (2004b) *Education*, www.library.cornell.edu/preservation/training/index.html.

Cox, R. J. (2000) The Great Newspaper Caper: backlash in the digital age, *First Monday*, **5** (12), http://firstmonday.org/issues/issue5_12/cox/index.html.

Craig-McFeely, J. and Deegan, M. (2005) Bringing the Digital Revolution to Medieval Musicology: the Digital Image Archive of Medieval Music (DIAMM), *RLG DigiNews*, **9** (3), www.rlg.org/en/page.php?Page_ID=20666#article1.

Cullen, B. T. (2000) *Authentication of Digital Objects: lessons from a historian's research*, Washington DC, Council on Library and Information Resources, www.clir.org/pubs/reports/pub92/cullen.html.

Deegan, M. and Tanner, S. (2002) *Digital Futures: strategies for the information age*, London, Library Association Publishing.

Digital Forensics Center (n.d.) *Digital Forensics Legal Summary*, University of Rhode Island, http://dfc.cs.uri.edu/resources/LegalSummary.html.

Kenney, A. (1997) The Cornell Digital to Microfilm Conversion Project: final report to NEH, *RLG Diginews*, **1** (2), www.rlg.org/legacy/preserv/diginews/diginews2.html#com.

MacKenzie, G. (2000), Searching for Solutions: electronic records problems worldwide, *Managing Information*, **7** (6), 59-65.

Pearson, D. (2000) Letter, *Times Literary Supplement*, (8 September).

RLG-OCLC (2002) *Trusted Digital Repositories: attributes and responsibilities, an RLG-OCLC report*, www.rlg.org/legacy/longterm/repositories.pdf.

Rothenberg, J. (2000) *Preserving Authentic Digital Information*, www.clir.org/pubs/reports/pub92/rothenberg.html.

# CHAPTER 5

# Moving with the times in search of permanence

Yola de Lusenet

## Introduction

Reformatting of library and archive materials is an established strategy to support access to and the preservation of collections. Its role in collection management follows, on the one hand, from the tasks and mission of the institution - the needs of its user communities, its role in the preservation of heritage - and, on the other, from the characteristics of the materials themselves, which may range from medieval parchment to videotapes, from a peace treaty carrying the original signatures of political leaders to recordings of animal sounds made for research purposes. In addition, there are other determining factors, such as available resources and priorities perceived by the public and politicians. The digital revolution has contributed to the spectrum of possibilities and has brought about a fundamental change in the relationship between reformatting, preservation and access.

The choice is not so hard in cases where preservation can be left out of the equation altogether. Reformatting for access nowadays inevitably means digitization, for its obvious advantages for distant access, possibilities for searching, re-use, copying, etc. This is not to say that digitization for access is without its problems. The technology is new and it still suffers from limitations - sometimes even at a basic level, with regard to presentation, speed, and quality - while aspects like rights, persistent identifiers, integrity and authenticity are far from being resolved. Anyone who has ever tried to view moving image files over the web, for instance, has experienced poor quality and the quirks of media players. However, most of these issues are not exclusive to the library and archive field, and as there are commercial interests at stake here, it is likely that improvements will be forthcoming from which the public sector can profit as well.

The choices are much less straightforward in the exclusive domain of the heritage sector, that is the management of collections for access and preservation for the long term. Whereas the potential of digitization to open up collections on an unprecedented scale is beyond dispute, its role as a reformatting option for preservation is controversial, in view of the many uncertainties associated with the long-term maintenance of digital materials. The broad attention this problem is now receiving inspires some confidence that solutions will be found, but it is not so clear whether approaches will be developed that fit the mission of memory institutions 'to keep materials for perpetuity' and that are also affordable.

In the midst of widespread enthusiasm for digitization, and of the rapid changes it brings, it is at the moment extremely hard for institutions that see themselves as part of a long tradition extending far into the future to make a balanced assessment of the possibilities and risks. There is serious pressure from the political arena – where time is characteristically measured by the distance between elections – to meet the constantly evolving needs of the information society, to serve users as befits a dynamic organization in the digital era, and to stimulate cultural participation of different groups of citizens. Then there is a huge responsibility for vast collections handed down over centuries that demands that stable solutions are chosen in a search for permanence. To reconcile these tasks, which are pulling institutions in different directions, would be difficult enough at the best of times. However, in the face of a constant and crippling lack of resources, establishing a well-founded strategy becomes more than just a challenge. Against this background any discussion of reformatting can only outline priorities and arguments that inform the choices made by institutions, in the full realization that for them the choice is all too often between the devil and the deep blue sea.

## Keeping things on paper

In the last decades of the 20th century the full scope of the problem of deteriorating paper materials from the 19th and 20th centuries came to be realized. Surveys have demonstrated it concerns enormous amounts of printed materials and many kilometres of archival documents: for instance, more than 33% of the holdings or 50 kms of shelving of records are threatened at the National Archives in the UK (Rhys-Lewis, 2001, 6). When one takes into account that compared to northwestern Europe, the conditions for paper production and storage have been far less favourable in many other parts of the world, a picture of a massive global problem emerges. For the printed heritage, which by definition exists in multiple copies, much can be gained by co-ordination and co-operation, but not a whole lot can be achieved in this way for archival holdings, which are mostly unique and must by law be kept by a specific repository. For the bulk of more recent materials, for which conservation is not a viable option, the choice is between on the one hand trying to slow down deterioration by optimal storage or deacidification of originals, or on the other to save their contents and reformat them.

## Microfilming

Microfilming has over the past half-century been the preferred reformatting strategy, and more popular than photocopying because it offers the possibility of further duplication. Preservation microfilming, according to current standards, involves making a master, a print copy from which further copies can be made, and user copies (for standards see, e.g., www.eromm.org/standards.htm, or www.metamorfoze.nl/publicaties/ richtlijnen/richtlijnen.html). As a master created according to standard has a life expectancy of hundreds of years if stored under environmentally controlled conditions, preservation of the content is ensured, whereas the possibilities for duplication at the same time give microfilming a role in increasing access. Microfilm registers such as EROMM (European Register of Microform Masters) have been set up so that institutions planning to reformat a specific work can check whether a master already exists elsewhere and, if so, request a service copy instead of making their own microform. For users, microfilm has long been the only possibility to gain access to information in documents not accessible to them in their original format, either because they are too valuable or too fragile to be consulted, or because they are kept at distant locations.

Although microfilm is widely supported in professional circles as a medium serving both preservation and access, it appears never to have been very popular with users. For many readers, access to originals is much to be preferred. Consulting an authentic document offers the experience of a direct link with the past, and in transfer to another medium, by definition not every characteristic of a document can be retained. Perhaps it is not considered very relevant for the type of use associated with, say, a 19th century scholarly journal that the original is reduced to a bitonal image in pure black and white, or that the binding can no longer be seen, but something is lost all the same. Moreover, most readers will simply find it easier and more comfortable to browse through paper books and documents.

However, as one of the explicit purposes of reformatting is to relieve strain on originals, as a rule readers are often referred first to microforms when these are available. This is inevitable if the materials must be kept in their original format, but when the primary goal is to preserve their *contents*, it is also possible to turn things around and take readers' preferences for consulting originals into account. The Bavarian State Library, for instance, places strong emphasis on access to originals and has made this a cornerstone in its policies. For certain items access to originals is provided even when they have been microfilmed. Post-1840 materials outside the core of the collections threatened by embrittlement, which are only important for the information they contain, are microfilmed to save their contents, and in keeping with the policy to preserve only one format (for these brittle books that format is microfilm) and to provide maximum access to originals, the print versions remain in circulation for as long as they last while the surrogates are stored under controlled conditions (Bavarian State Library, 2005).

The Bavarian State Library, which goes back to 1558 and holds over 8 million volumes and substantial special collections, including important manuscript collections, is a typical example of an institution with a long tradition that has to combine (legal) tasks for the preservation of national or regional heritage (in this case the printed heritage of Bavaria) with services for a wide community of users (i.e., students and researchers). For institutions like these, microfilming has long been a viable reformatting strategy and it is still regarded as the strategy of choice for preservation, even if it has fallen from grace in recent years as a way to increase access.

A recent report from the National Preservation Office of the UK and Ireland that investigated the role of microfilming concludes that 'microfilming to archival standards is still very much part of the preservation solution palette – despite the availability of funding for digital options' (Rhys-Lewis, 2005, 2). The report underlines that 'the ongoing development of hybrid solutions – combining the effective elements of both the microfilm and digitisation processes – [is] vital to ensuring that microfilm [processed to archival standards] remains a viable preservation option' (2005, 7).

## Hybrid approaches

So-called hybrid approaches, in which microfilm and scanned images are created in one two-step process, have been explored for quite some time, and guidelines for producing preservation microfilm for scanning have been published by the Research Libraries Group (2003). These guidelines meet a need as in projects for digitizing existing microfilms it has been found that older films are not in all respects of sufficient quality to be digitized without problems, especially if one of the aims is to generate searchable text with optical character recognition (OCR). But if microfilm is produced to standard, the two-step process with scanning from microfilm is now an economical approach that results in high-quality images.

The combination is especially attractive when the original materials make direct scanning less straightforward, as is the case with newspapers. Experience with digitization of (existing) microfilms of newspapers has been gained in recent years in several large projects. Newspapers have often been microfilmed in the past, not only with a view to the preservation of material printed on low-quality paper – fragile and easily damaged through handling by the combination of high use and large format – but also to facilitate storage and distribution. For their value as historical sources for research and their direct appeal for a large group of interested users, newspapers are prime candidates for digitization. Moreover, sophisticated software is now available to produce text for searching even from pages with a complex newspaper layout. The projects that are underway in Europe – for instance at the Koninklijke Bibliotheek, the national library of the Netherlands,

'Kranten in beeld' (http://kranten.kb.nl/index.html); in the Nordic countries the joint TIDEN project (http://tiden.kb.se/); and at the British Library (www.bl.uk/collections/britishnewspapers1800to1900.html – have produced various websites offering different solutions for the presentation and searching of hundreds of thousands of pages of newspapers. The TIDEN project has worked with the International Federation of Library Associations and Institutions (IFLA) on a supplement to the guidelines for preservation microfilming of newspapers which deals with special requirements for OCR (IFLA, 1996, 2002).

So far, scanning microfilm seems more widespread in the heritage sector than the reverse procedure, that is digitizing first and producing microfilm from digital images (Computer Output Microfilm). This may be due to familiarity with microfilming processes and standards, which makes it easier for institutions to set up an efficient workflow, deal with external vendors, and ensure adequate quality control when they start with filming. This route may also have been chosen because existing microfilms could be used in the project. In the end, however, it is more important *that* microfilming and digitization are combined in reformatting strategies than *how* they are combined. The basis for a hybrid approach is the recognition that in the paper environment there are now two reformatting strategies which each have their strengths and can complement each other. As the IFLA Newspapers Section (2002) puts it: 'If a quality program for microfilming is established as a part of the library strategy, it will make things easier for the future digitisation activities. Microfilming should be considered as a part of the library's digital program.'

The rationale for this approach is threefold. First, heritage institutions should ensure that for deteriorating materials a stable surrogate is created. Second, it is often easier and cheaper to digitize from the surrogate than from the originals. Third, digital images created now may well prove to be temporary, not only due to the difficulty of preserving digital files, but also because it is quite possible that at some time in the future evolving technology may result in higher demands for digital presentation than can be realized at the moment. For funders and decision makers, the arguments for economy, efficiency and future possibilities may be the stronger ones, but for the heritage sector the creation of a reliable intermediary that can serve as a preservation surrogate is equally essential.

The rapid development of web technology serves to support the idea that the digital materials we create now may not be what we will need in 50 years' time. On the contrary, if we go by the revolutions in the recording and distribution of information over the past century, it is more than likely that we will need something entirely different. This justifies a cautious approach that keeps all options open. Preservation, though it is often seen as preoccupation with rescuing things from the past, is in fact oriented towards the future in that it is concerned with sustainability issues. Heritage institutions characteristically hold vast amounts of materials, part of which they are legally bound to keep irrespective of their use and even when access to them is restricted, and they cannot rely solely on digitization, which is essentially driven by requirements for present access. Their reformatting policies necessarily have to distinguish between short-term and long-term goals.

In a comprehensive reformatting strategy, microfilm and digitization can be positioned in different ways. High-quality microfilm can figure as a stable intermediary that can be used for rescanning just in case, and also when originals are not in any way endangered. When preservation is an issue, the microfilm can be seen as the preservation medium that also serves as a starting point for digitization for access. The digital files then have to meet current requirements but they do not necessarily have to be created with a view to permanence. After all, building a sustainable digital environment for the long term does not by definition coincide with the requirements of present users. Creating files that may not survive technological change can be a responsible decision stemming from a modest acknowledgement that we cannot know how user expectations will evolve and which content will be the most relevant for future generations. In this view, creating digital files that can be kept for perpetuity requires serious investment that may well turn out to be wasted if interests move in other directions.

## Digital preservation

Meanwhile, that every effort should be made to build a sustainable digital environment is another matter. The question here is whether all materials now being digitized have a place there and whether it is at all possible to maintain all digitized materials. For the time being digital preservation is considered to be many times more expensive than preservation of analogue media. The costs of storage media go down by the day, but this effect is counteracted by an exponential growth in the need for storage space and the cost of complex infrastructure for managing huge amounts of data: not so much the costs of hardware as software and staff to maintain the system. Stephen Chapman (2003) presented figures on storage costs a couple of years ago, and even if the exact figures are no longer entirely up to date, his conclusion still stands that digital storage is many times more expensive than analogue storage. Digital *preservation*, on the other hand, includes a lot more than storage: anecdotal evidence suggests that storage costs are now in the area of £2 to £4 sterling per gigabyte, whereas the costs of storing microfilm in a vault are very modest. In these circumstances there are good arguments for a strategy that relies on microfilm as a preservation medium and uses digitization to improve access, without any claims for the long term.

The arguments for such a dual approach are even stronger when one considers the huge size of the holdings in the heritage sector and the large proportion of materials that is only sporadically used or not used at all, but still needs to be preserved. Projects for digitization now completed or underway at the British Library will, for instance, result in a couple of years in a total of 3 million images, which is a lot but still only 0.2% of the collection (Shenton, 2004, 70). A recent European Union (EU) document published in support of a highly ambitious strategy for digital libraries in Europe firmly states that 'digitisation and online libraries initiatives have to be rooted in demand and use' and, a little further on, 'European libraries hold in total more than 2.5 billion (2,500 million) books and bound periodicals. Not all of these books are unique, but even digitising all the unique material would be practically impossible' (European Commission, 2005).

This must surely be read as an understatement: from the principle that the European digital library should be 'rooted in demand and use', it inevitably follows that it will only include a *fraction* of the total collections. It is a vision of a library that bears more resemblance to a public library than to a large research library with specialist collections or a deposit library that has to take care of the national printed heritage. This does not detract from the idea as such, but it does point to the need for maintaining and providing access to the paper heritage in other ways as well.

For low-use materials and materials they are legally bound to keep in any case, archives and libraries may well choose to focus on preservation – of originals or contents – and rely on microfilm as a stable and relatively cheap technology, particularly for 19th- and 20th-century text-based documents. For archives especially, microfilm has the added advantage that it does not raise questions as to authenticity and integrity, as digital copies do, a phenomenon that is bringing about a shift in archival practice which has always been defined by the existence of known categories of physical, tangible documents. Many specialist materials will not be digitized, or will be scanned only on request. Other materials for which there is known or potential interest may be converted from the original or microfilm into true digital formats – with added functionality for searching, zooming and copying – and some may survive successive digital environments. Others will be recreated at some later stage according to requirements that are as yet unknown. A combination of approaches offers the best prospects for continued access to a massive and varied printed heritage that has different user groups with different expectations.

It should be borne in mind that it has taken several decades to develop responsible procedures for microfilming to meet preservation requirements. The availability of technology is not enough: a whole complex of standards and processes needs to be built, for specifications and quality control, for storage and handling, for decisions about retaining originals, and with expert staff who understand why these things matter. In the midst of an information revolution, it is easy to be carried along on the wide road to the bright digital future. But then history may well repeat itself: 'If we have not learned anything from our microfilming mistakes, we will waste enormous amounts of money and serve scholars poorly. The digitizing must be done well to be useful, and we must be able to ensure the preservation of electronic formats that may be even more ephemeral than newsprint' (Wittenborg, 2001).

## Images or objects

The world of photographs is even less stable than that of texts, as photography is a chemical process and all photographs are subject to intrinsic decay that is on the whole more pronounced than paper degradation. Because so many different photographic processes and materials have been used, the exact chemical composition of individual photographs is often not known. Some processes have proven to be very unstable, such as acetate film and early colour photography. In addition, environmental factors, such as fluctuating temperature and humidity, greatly accelerate the process of deterioration.

The photographic heritage is in many respects more threatened by decay than the paper heritage, and has for decades been seriously neglected, for instance because in many archives photographs were not regarded as records worth preserving, but as documentation. Although there is a limited number of dedicated (national) institutions for photography, there is nothing like the institutional infrastructure supporting the management of collections of books and journals or archival paper records. Photographic collections are found in many types of institution, often as a minority collection managed along the lines of the rest of the holdings. There are no widely used descriptive standards specifically developed for photographic collections, and many collections are poorly described. The situation for European photographic collections has been described by Klijn and de Lusenet (2000).

Reformatting of photographs for preservation and access has only really taken off with the advent of digital technology and the web. Duplication is used to create photographic copies, for preservation or on request, and microfilm has been used for reference copies of low quality, but there were no large-scale reformatting programmes comparable to microfilming of paper materials. Digitization of photographs has been enthusiastically taken up by the heritage sector as historical photographs constitute an important cultural resource that lends itself easily to presentation on the web. Digitization also came at the right time in that interest in photographic collections was growing, and there was considerable interest on the part of researchers and the general public to gain access to materials that up till then had been mostly hidden from view.

To many, reformatting of photographs also seemed unproblematic as even a simple scanner can produce what is often considered an adequate image, without interference by experts. Most of such digital images bear only a faint resemblance to the originals in the eyes of specialists, who understand a photograph as a cultural artefact, whereas the average user will be inclined to equate the visual image with the photograph. This raises questions as to the position and value of originals, the chances of their preservation, and the status of the digital copies.

In terms of materiality, an image on a screen and a photographic print are essentially different, and transfer to another medium creates another object. By definition, the characteristics of the photographic object cannot be translated into a digital equivalent, and in this view ultimately a digital image can never be more than a visual reference to an original. One can achieve an excellent representation of a *picture*, partly with reference to objective targets to measure how much information is captured (level of detail, how many shades of grey). Yet, even here ethical considerations come into play: should the photograph as it is now be reproduced as closely as possible, or can effects of deterioration such as fading be 'reversed' through image processing, to come closer to the intent of the photographer at the time? This is familiar terrain for those working with historical photographic collections, where different prints of the same negative may exist, produced by different hands, or the negative, the most direct recording of the original scene, may differ considerably from the print the photographer chose to make in the end. When a press photograph has been severely cropped for maximum effect, does one refer to the uncropped negative or the cropped print? Decisions on such issues vary from case to case and are usually informed by the nature of the material and the professional ethics of the conservators and curators involved. For documentary collections that are primarily seen as sources of information, the decisions may well be different than for photographs regarded as cultural artefacts or as fine art.

As photographs function in so many different ways, digitization of photographs brings a number of issues to the fore that are much less prominent in the reformatting of textual sources, which are mostly treated as information (with obvious exceptions, such as illuminated manuscripts) and for which a lot has been conventionalized in decades of microfilming. It is not at all clear to what extent digitization of photographs should be seen as reformatting in the sense of creating a surrogate that is meant to be a substitute for the original. Fine art prints and valuable historical photographs will no doubt survive for quite some time as originals, with digital copies functioning like visual references or for distribution, much like photographs published in books. But for many photographs valued for their content, almost inevitably the digital copies will take over most or all of the functions of the originals, which, at best, are safely stored under climatized conditions after digitization. Assuming that digital preservation will somehow be dealt with, in the end digital copies will then, in practice, be all we have and know.

However, as the production and reception of photographs is often inscribed in their materiality, their authenticity rests all too often in clues that are not part of the image itself, but can only be read from the material that is left behind in reformatting. Translating such information into metadata accompanying the image is a vital step in a reformatting process. Given the unstable nature of the digital object – easily corrupted in migration and open to invisible change, whether accidentally or intentionally – it remains doubtful whether even extensively documented digital images can ever become true substitutes for all possible uses. In their role as evidential records and sources for historical research, photographs may have to remain accessible in the original as well, for as long as possible. They may even be consulted more than before when their existence can be easily established through digitized collections on the web.

## The information, not the carrier

'Audiovisual' is used in this section to refer to audio and video collections only; usually the term covers film as well, but as reformatting and digitization have a very different position in management of film collections than for video and audio, this discussion is limited to audio and video. For audio and video collections preservation and long-term access depend entirely on reformatting. Audio and video carriers are fragile – disks are easily broken or scratched – and/or inherently unstable, such as many types of magnetic tape. More importantly, they become obsolete as they depend on machines to be used, and this machine-dependency defines strategies for preservation and access. According to some estimates, two-thirds of the materials cannot now be easily used, and through decay and obsolescence in the best scenario 40% of the tape-based content may be lost by 2045; in the worst scenario this may be even 70% by 2025 (Addis and Miller, 2005).

With audiovisual we enter a realm where carriers are merely functional, just temporary means to store information so that it can be represented with the help of some device, without any artefactual value. (Although sound records have become collectibles, also for their sleeves and labels, for preservation and access their contents will still need to be transferred.) In this respect the audiovisual world is a precursor of the digital environment, with carriers and equipment succeeding each other and phasing out previous generations. For analogue audio and video materials, the changes have been slower, but still so fast that considerable amounts of materials have become practically inaccessible and wide-scale reformatting has become urgent (IASA Technical Committee, 2001; Wright, 2004).

Another similarity with the digital environment is that change is strongly driven by interest to explore new consumer markets or commercial applications in the music industry or broadcasting. The technology changes in audio and video have created a cycle in which specialisms in industry are being lost by the time they are needed in the heritage sector to deal with the materials left in its care. When one considers the transfer period for archival materials is in most countries several decades, it will be clear that archives in general receive audiovisual materials when the format is already obsolete and equipment in short supply, while technicians who can handle it have mostly been retrained or are retired.

Interest in the audiovisual heritage has increased only recently, partly because the broadcasting industry itself has taken up the issue. Broadcasters are experiencing serious problems in the re-use of their massive archives held on obsolete formats, and for efficient management and continued access they are eager to digitize their holdings. Large EU programmes have in recent years explored large-scale approaches to 'digital preservation' of audiovisual collections, most notably Presto and its successor Presto-Space (www.prestospace.org/).

Broadcasters use the term 'digital preservation' in a slightly different sense from librarians and archivists, to refer to the process of the conversion from analogue to digital, with a view to managing digital resources in mass-storage systems. Sound archivists particularly, though they favour conversion to digital as the only viable long-term solution for keeping sound materials alive, are often somewhat wary of the use of the term 'preservation' in this context. Their concern is that quality standards acceptable to broadcasting – where re-use is the primary motive for digitization – do not constitute true preservation of all the information contained in the originals. The International Association of Sound Archives (IASA) has published guidelines for digitization of audio to preservation standards, which bring out the complexity of achieving optimal signal extraction from the variety of carriers threatened by decay or obsolescence (Bradley, 2004). There is, however, consensus that digitization is the only option to guarantee continued access to the audio heritage, and conversion is now possible at relatively low cost to an open, standard format (buf, wav).

For video, the situation is somewhat different as there is as yet no open, agreed standard that meets preservation standards, but the digital environment brings the same advantages for audio and video in terms of improved access and possibilities of endless copying without loss of quality, which is not possible in the analogue domain. As digitization will take many years to accomplish, storage of originals under climatized conditions to extend their useful life, and acquisition and maintenance of replay equipment remain essential to ensure access for the coming years. Ultimately, the analogue environment cannot be maintained, and strategies to keep it alive for as long as possible are to be seen as efforts to stretch the available time for conversion. Although some of the equipment will no doubt survive into the future and some carriers – such as shellac disks – may, if carefully handled, still be playable, it is unrealistic to rely on possibilities for freezing analogue systems for large collections. If it could work for preservation, it certainly would not work for access, which for audiovisual collections has never been optimal anyway.

A survey carried out in 2005, on the situation of audiovisual collections in Europe, shows that in many heritage institutions where audiovisual materials constitute a minority collection, access is hindered by incomplete cataloguing and lack of replay equipment. The results also indicate that many institutions are hesitant to undertake digitization of their audiovisual collections, sometimes because they may underestimate the risks to analogue carriers, but more often out of concern about the instability of the digital domain. The survey was part of the TAPE (Training for Audiovisual Preservation in Europe) project, funded by the Culture 2000 programme of the EU and co-ordinated by the European Commission on Preservation and Access (www.tape-online.net) (for the situation of audio collections in academic libraries in the USA, see Smith et al., 2004). It is understandable that institutions in search of permanence are daunted by the prospects sketched by broadcasters: heavily automated mass-storage systems for managing huge amounts of digital data; with replacement cycles for data tape media and drives of three to five years; where migration has to be a continuous activity; and full-spread redundancy (several copies, technologies and locations) is essential. For heritage institutions that are beginning to get worried about the survival of their analogue holdings, the message that the future is in mass storage that 'cannot be trusted but must be managed' will sound like an encouragement to jump from the frying pan into the fire.

## Conclusions

In the end, whether continued access to the cultural heritage can be guaranteed may not depend so much on the choice of specific reformatting strategies as on the broader question as to how the heritage sector will be positioned in the digital environment and to what extent they will be able to shape this environment themselves. Bold statements about the digital future may sometimes strike those in the heritage world as frivolous or perhaps even apocalyptic. Reports in the 1980s and 1990s of the demise of the book turned out to be greatly exaggerated, and similarly, now that we are presented with visions of universal web access and empty libraries without walls, these could be dismissed as wishful thinking under the argument that it is impossible for heritage institutions to digitize all their holdings. This may be true, but it may also turn out to be irrelevant.

These not-so-futuristic visions may well become a reality, not because everything that could be used is digitized, but because only what is digital will be used. Even now, when only a minute fraction of the total analogue holdings is accessible online, the internet generation now entering universities relies first and foremost on Google for their information. Preservation professionals are worrying that what is digital may be lost; others believe that what is not digital will most certainly be lost, not perhaps in a material sense, but in an intellectual one, as a link in the tradition that has disappeared from sight, even if it still exists somewhere on a shelf in a library or archive.

In the end, it may prove to be less decisive for the future information environment what the heritage world is digitizing or reformatting or otherwise trying to keep accessible than what others are doing. Digitization by the heritage sector is already now being dwarfed by the efforts in the commercial sector to bring information to the web. The large science publishers are digitizing their back volumes of the journal literature, and the same material that research libraries have bought in the past through subscriptions and are committed to keep is now being resold to the same libraries through licences for access to digitized versions – access without ownership. Corbis is buying up the visual heritage and reselling it in digital format. And most recently giants like Google, Microsoft and Yahoo have moved in to digitize complete libraries. Google's plan is to digitize substantive parts of the holdings of five major libraries, and all the 7.4 million books of the University of Michigan they hope to convert within six years, a feat that would have taken Michigan 1,400 years at its present rate of digitizing (*NRC Handelsblad*, 2005). To many it is the aggregation of large amounts of information that will offer opportunities for truly innovative research, and commercial companies are now rapidly aggregating all they can lay their hands on. Donald Waters (2005, 11) has presented what he considers a plausible scenario:

(1) Libraries will not own the publications that form the scholarly record; (2) libraries will not own the archive of the scholarly record; and (3) publishers

will charge whatever the market can bear for data-mining services because they control all the underlying resources. In other words, if universities and libraries fail to act responsibly and soon in creating archives of electronic journals and other scholarly resources, and publishers act instead, the way will be clear for them to complete a massive transfer of wealth and control over the scholarly record.

Waters's paper deals with the future of scholarly publishing and information, but the scenario he sketches may apply equally to all heritage materials. As the fierce debate around the 'Google 5' reveals (Bailey (2005) presents an overview of responses; see also Brandt (2005) and Lavoie et al. (2005)), in the end access and preservation will depend more on ownership, rights, sustainability of digital collections, and the added services that can be developed, than on who digitizes what. As Waters said in a response to the Google agreement, 'digitizing is just scratching the surface' (Roush, 2005): there remains a lot more to be done in order to make extensive and distributed digital collections truly accessible and to also maintain optimal access in the future. In the present information revolution, the keepers of our documentary and intellectual heritage have to carve out a role for themselves to ensure that, not only in theory but also in practice, access remains wide and varied, supporting principles of freedom of information and traditions of research that are the basis of our society. The stakes may be higher than ever before, but the dilemma is still to keep what we have come to rely on, while making a transition to new access and use, 'to be both extraordinarily innovative and conservative at the same time' (Waters, 2005, 21).

## References

[URLs accessed 11 December 2005.]

Addis, M. and Miller, A. (2005) *Cost Models for Digitisation and Storage of Audiovisual Archives, paper presented at the DCC/DPC Workshop on Cost Models for Preserving Digital Assets, London, 26 July 2005*, www.dpconline.org/docs/events/050726psxpiti.pdf.

Bailey, C. W., Jr (2005) *The Google Print Controversy: a bibliography*, a Scholarly Electronic Publishing weblog, www.escholarlypub.com/digitalkoans/2005/10/25/the-google-print-controversy-a-bibliography/.

Bavarian State Library (2005) *Abteilung für Informationssicherung und Bestandserhaltung*, www.bsb-muenchen.de/.

Bradley, K. (ed.) (2004) *Guidelines on the Production and Preservation of Digital Audio Objects*, Auckland Park, South Africa, International Association of Sound and Audiovisual Archives.

Brandt, D. (2005) Google-Eyed U. Michigan Gives Away its Library, (19 June), www.google-watch.org/umich.html.

Chapman, S. (2003) Counting the Costs of Digital Preservation: is repository storage affordable?, *Journal of Digital Information*, 4 (2), http://jodi.ecs.soton.ac.uk/Articles/v04/i02/Chapman/.

European Commission (2005) *European Digital Libraries: frequently asked questions*, Press release 30 September 2005 MEMO/05/347, http://europa.eu/comm/press_room/index_en.htm.

IASA Technical Committee (2001) *The Safeguarding of the Audio Heritage: ethics, principles and preservation strategy*, International Association of Sound Archives, www.iasa-web.org/iasa0013.htm.

IFLA, Round Table on Newspapers/IFLA Section on Serial Publications (1996) *Guidelines for Newspaper Preservation Microfilming*, IFLA Professional Reports No. 49, The Hague, International Federation of Library Associations, www.ifla.org/VII/s39/broch/pr49-e.pdf.

IFLA, Newspapers Section (2002) *Microfilming for Digitisation and Optical Character Recognition Supplement to Guideline*, www.ifla.org/VII/s39/broch/microfilming.htm.

Klijn, E. and de Lusenet, Y. (2000) *In the Picture: preservation and digitisation of European photographic collections*, Amsterdam, European Commission on Preservation and Access, www.knaw.nl/ecpa/publ/pdf/885.pdf.

Lavoie, B., Connaway, L. S. and Dempsey, L. (2005) Anatomy of Aggregate Collections: the example of Google Print for Libraries, *D-Lib Magazine*, 11 (9), www.dlib.org/dlib/september05/lavoie/09lavoie.html.

*NRC Handelsblad* (2005) Studenten Zoeken Niet in Boeken [Students Do Not Search in Books], *NRC Handelsblad*, (25 November).

Research Libraries Group (2003) *RLG Guidelines for Microfilming to Support Digitization. Supplement to RLG Microfilming Publications*, Research

Libraries Group, www.rlg.org/preserv/microsuppl.pdf.

Rhys-Lewis, J. (2001) *The Enemy Within: acid deterioration of our written heritage,* a report to the British Library Co-operation and Partnership Programme, London, www.bl.uk/services/npo/pdf/infosave.html.

Rhys-Lewis, J. (2005) *A Report on a Recent Review of Preservation Microfilming Carried out by Libraries and Archives across the UK and Ireland,* London, National Preservation Office, www.bl.uk/services/npo/pdf/microfilm.pdf.

Roush, W. (2005) The Infinite Library: does Google's plan to digitize millions of print books spell the death of libraries, or their rebirth? *Technology Review,* (May), www.technologyreview.com/read_article.aspx?id=14408&ch=infotech.

Shenton, H. (2004) Managing the Life Cycle Decisions for the Long-term Use of Original Collection Material and Surrogates. In Webster, J., *'Parallel Lives': Digital and Analog Options for Access and Preservation, papers given at the joint conference of the National Preservation Office and King's College London, 10 November 2003,* London, National Preservation Office/British Library.

Smith, A., Allen, D. R. and Allen, K. (2004) *Survey of the State of Audio Collections in Academic Libraries,* Washington DC, Council on Library and Information Resources, www.clir.org/pubs/abstract/pub128abst.html.

Waters, D. J. (2005) *Managing Digital Assets in Higher Education: an overview of strategic issues (a work in progress), paper presented at the conference Managing Digital Assets: Strategic Issues for Research Libraries, Washington DC, 28 October 2005,* www.arl.org/forum05/#proceedings.

Wittenborg, K. (2001) *A Librarian Looks at Preservation, paper presented at the conference Do We Want to Keep our Newspapers?, University of London, 12–13 March,* www.arl.org/preserv/wittenborg.html.

Wright, R. (2004), Digital Preservation of Audio, Video and Film, *VINE: The Journal of Information and Knowledge Management Systems,* **34** (2), 71–6.

# CHAPTER 6

# Valuation model for paper conservation research: a new approach for setting research priorities

Henk J. Porck, Frank J. Ligterink, Gerrit de Bruin and Steph Scholten

[Preservation is] the management of risks to collections to restrict the rate of loss of collection value to an optimum, low level. (Waller, 2003)

[Conservation is] the management of resources, especially but not exclusively, material cultural resources, to prolong the lifetime of material culture, to enhance usability, and to clarify contained messages of various kinds for the continuance and betterment of humanity. (Rosvall et al., 1995)

[Conservation research is] the generation of knowledge that can be applied to achieve a maximum effective collection value through optimisation of the combination of preservation of and access to a collection as a whole, under a given conservation budget. (this chapter)

## Introduction

The preservation and conservation of cultural heritage collections are core activities of libraries, archives and museums. They are recognized as important issues that require significant resources. Conservation research, carried out in many locations all over the world by a variety of researchers, forms an integral part of conservation policies. Knowledge generated by conservation research is necessary to underpin sound decision making. Actors involved in conservation research range from specialized conservation scientists and conservators to students of conservation colleges and professionals in related, sometimes industrial, research disciplines. Their work is condensed into an expanding body of literature and knowledge.

It must be recognized that the incentive for conservation research does not always originate from the objective of collection preservation only. The involvement in research of commercial companies may, for example, be motivated by public relations concerns. Non-commercial research institutes almost always act in political environments that may influence the conservation research agenda. We should be aware that these external forces do introduce a risk of biased research. In practice it can be difficult to recognize this potential bias. It is interesting to see, as an example, how and to what extent a major funding programme, such as that of the European Union, has influenced directions in conservation research by importing its political ambitions in research programmes. An overview of several developments and certain 'trends' in conservation science is presented in Porck and Teygeler (2000). Another external motive for conservation research (i.e., not instigated by the goal of preservation), is pure scientific curiosity. Scientific curiosity is definitely a vital driving force for any research, but is also difficult to control. At some point research may become an aim in itself and will get detached from its original goals. For instance, how many specialized analytical tools for the characterization of cultural objects have not been developed by conservation scientists without a clear and proper application purpose?

However justified these remarks may be, the role of conservation science as such should not be disputed. If serious amounts of money are spent on intervention or preventive conservation measures within local or national preservation programmes, it is wise to reserve some part of the resources to review and evaluate the strategies used and to look for possible improvements and new directions. It is important that this reviewing, evaluating and searching is done in a rigorous, independent and objective manner, taking into account both the benefits and costs involved. This approach constitutes its scientific character and forms the basis for our definition of conservation science, that is the generation of knowledge to support the efficient use of resources in order to optimize the preservation of and access to our cultural heritage.

Within the framework of the Dutch national programme for the preservation of library and archival materials, *Metamorfoze*, three national institutions – Instituut Collectie Nederland (ICN, Netherlands Institute for Cultural Heritage), the Koninklijke Bibliotheek (KB, National Library of the Netherlands) and the Nationaal Archief (NA, National Archives of the Netherlands) – have been given the joint responsibility to co-ordinate a national programme for paper conservation research for the years 2004 to 2008. A first step in the design of this programme has been the development of a valuation model for paper conservation research. This model is primarily based on the idea that different research options can be evaluated and prioritized beforehand by quantitatively estimating their associated 'success' in improving the preservation of and access to Dutch paper-based collections in a most cost-effective way. In this chapter, the term 'collections' is used for groups of documents and/or other paper artefacts in libraries, archives and museums. The framework, elaboration and discussion of the Valuation Model for Paper Conservation Research ('Valuation Model', in short), will be presented in this chapter.

## Valuation model for paper conservation research
### Scope
The focus of conservation research is traditionally determined by the universal and central importance attached by the field to the subject of material knowledge. This includes knowledge of historic materials, production processes and users' practices, as well as modern conservation and restoration materials and techniques. Each new research programme is based on state-of-the-art material knowledge and expertise. Against this background, the objective of paper conservation science – the generation of knowledge to support the efficient use of resources in order to optimize the preservation of and access to our paper cultural heritage – can be further elaborated. 'Our paper cultural heritage' primarily addresses the written, drawn and printed paper artefacts collected and stored in archives, libraries and museums.

Within this context, the crucial role of collection managers should be stressed. New research and new knowledge can only influence the preservation of and access to collections if collection managers actually apply research results in their policies and activities. Usually, a limited amount of free resources is available for preservation and access activities and services. The 'freedom of movement' in the use of these resources mainly applies to the choice for certain specific activities and investments in the areas of (1) preventive conservation measures, (2) conservation and restoration treatments, and (3) valuation and selection for conservation. Conservation research should be aimed at generating strategic, applicable knowledge in these three areas, enabling collection managers to establish a more efficient and effective resource management. Research can be directed towards development of new methods, instruments and materials, but also towards evaluation and improvement of already existing facilities and working procedures. Whereas preservation of and access to a collection are usually treated separately, often as conflicting factors, the scope of conservation research within the framework of the Valuation Model includes both aspects in a combined, integrated way.

## Testing and prioritizing

The field of conservation research, as sketched above, is very broad and diverse. It includes an extensive variety of subjects, each with its own historical background, argumentation and research methodology. This wide spectrum involves studies that seem incompatible. For example, a study of a technique to monitor the optical characteristics of archival documents during exhibition appears to be of a completely different nature from research on a suitable deacidification method for coated papers. On first glance this seems to be an insurmountable obstacle in the development of a coherent conservation research programme. However, the solution for this problem lies in keeping in mind the common goal – the generation of knowledge to improve preservation and access. Explicit valuation of research options in terms of their contribution to this goal will allow for well-considered prioritization as well as provide a guiding principle for the design of research proposals.

## Designation and definition of success indicators

Conservation research can contribute to realizing the desired objective in three distinct ways: research results can lead to an improvement of (1) preservation, (2) access and (3) economy (the saving of expenses). By formulating and applying quantitative indicators for the success expected in these three aspects, a ranking score can be given to any research proposal. The actual judgement of the expected success of a certain research option, according to the Valuation Model, is done by an *ex ante* estimation of the effects that can be reached at maximum.

Of course, the true success, the eventual impact of research, can only be established after the actual implementation of the research results. Beforehand, the outcome of the research itself is uncertain, nor do we know in advance if collection managers will decide to apply the research results. Therefore, the maximum effect of a certain research option is estimated *ex ante* under the conditions that the research in question succeeds, that is generates the desired knowledge, and that this knowledge is also actually put into practice.

### Preservation

An overarching conceptual framework for the quantification of the success factor 'preservation' is the Cultural Property Risk Analysis Model, developed by Robert Waller of the Canadian Museum of Nature (Waller, 2003). This methodology provides a comprehensive system in which all possible threats for collections are expressed as quantitative risks. The system distinguishes ten different generic risks: (1) physical forces, (2) fire, (3) water, (4) contaminants, (5) incorrect relative humidity, (6) incorrect temperature, (7) criminals, (8) pests, (9) light and UV radiation, and (10) dissociation, that is inaccessibility and loss of objects/data. An essential element in the calculation of the risks is the quantification of the (expected) loss of value of the collection materials as a consequence of specific damage processes connected with the various risk factors. This approach enables a mutual comparison of strongly different types of risk. The formula used in the risk assessment analysis is as follows:

$$MR = FS \times LV \times P \times E$$

MR: *Magnitude of Risk*, the quantitative measure of a certain risk

FS: *Fraction Susceptible*, the fraction of the collection that is vulnerable to the risk

LV: *Loss of Value*, the loss of value in 100 years, expressed as a fraction of the initial value

P: *Probability*, the likelihood that the risk occurs in the course of 100 years

E: *Extent*, how much of the potential damage connected with the risk actually becomes manifest

On the basis of the risk assessment methodology, the indicator 'preservation' ( $\Pi$, pi) can now be defined as the fraction of the current collection value (set at 1) that is expected to remain after the lapse of 100 years:

$$\Pi = 1 - MR$$

## Access

The second indicator for success of a research project deals with the improvement of access to the collection, which is achieved by the application of the knowledge generated by that research. Improvement of access can be reached in very different ways, for example by an increased physical resistance to handling or an improvement of the 'readability'. The latter may literally be the intensification of a faded writing ink on a document, but may also relate to the increase of material knowledge about an artefact, thus providing a more meaningful context.

Access to a collection depends of course on the organization's facilities that allow for direct or indirect consultation of the collection. The access level of a collection can be characterized by a relatively universal set of five access facilities:

L: *Listing*, access via a catalogue or an inventory list containing basic data

O: *Online presentation*, access by means of electronic full-text/image files

D: *Display possibilities*, consultation through physical exhibition of collection materials

R: *Reading room service*, consultation of original documents in the reading room

I: *Intellectual retrieval*, access via reading aids or documentary and material information

Usually, these facilities are offered rather independently of each other. In the calculation, each facility will be given a value between 0 and 1, indicating to what extent (fraction) the actual level of this facility meets the desired optimum. The access level (A) of a collection, expressed as a figure between 0 and 1, can thus be calculated as the sum of the individual facility levels, divided by 5:

$$A = (L + O + D + R + I) / 5$$

## Economy

The relevance of conservation research cannot be judged properly without considering the aspect of costs. In the Valuation Model, the costs considered do not refer to the costs of the conservation research itself, but specifically concern the expenses involved in the implementation of the research results in the conservation practice. In some cases, research is not directly aimed at improving preservation or access, but primarily concentrated on improving efficiency of already existing conservation activities. Conversely, if improved preservation or access is expected as an outcome when introducing a new conservation measure or method, the positive effect should be weighed against a possible increase in costs. These extra expenses include at least (1) the short-term immediate costs of implementation of research results and, if the application of the research results needs to be maintained for a longer period, (2) the long-term or structural costs.

Unlike the success indicators 'preservation' and 'access', the indicator 'economy' is not separately defined in the Valuation Model. As will be shown in the next section, the influence of the aspect of costs on the success of conservation research will be taken into account in an integrated manner.

## Weighing of success indicators
### Effective collection value

Our first experiences with the use of the Valuation Model have indicated that the three success indicators 'preservation', 'access' and 'economy' form a complete, comprehensive set. Discussing diverging arguments pro or contra certain research options has shown us that all can be categorized under one of the three indicators. The problem that subsequently must be faced is the question of how improvements in preservation, access and economy should be mutually weighed and integrated. Is it possible to compare research that leads to improved preservation with research improving access or resulting in more cost-effective conservation treatments?

To answer this question, it must be made clear first of all that preservation *in itself* and access *in itself* are not individual goals. The value of a collection only becomes effective in its use, in the interaction with its intended audience. There is, or should be, no collection manager putting much effort into preservation, without imagining that happy user at the moment of discovery of that single valuable, long wished-for document. On the other hand, access to a collection by exhibitions, for example, can never exist without the basic precondition of preservation of the collection. Adequate preservation – meaning the physical survival of a valuable collection – as well as proper access facilities allowing for sufficient consultation possibilities are equal and necessary conditions for optimal direct and long-term use of a collection. Given the objective of conservation research, as formulated before, it is the *combination* of preservation *and* access that counts. Following this line of reasoning, we define the 'effective collection value' (*V*) as the product of preservation and access. *V* can thus be calculated by multiplication of the success indicators $\Pi$ and $A$:

$$V = \Pi \times A$$

Nor is saving of costs a goal in itself. If, by the implementation of research results, specific conservation treatments can be performed at half the price, and the saved budget can be used for budget cuts or higher salaries for senior management for example, this would mean a loss, not a profit, from the viewpoint of preservation. The starting point for our model should be that savings flow back into the conservation budget. Conversely, new conservation measures demanding extra investments are also expected to come from that budget. Although conservation budgets will certainly vary in practice, the choice of a constant budget for our Valuation Model is considered to be a neutral, easily defensible simplification of a complex reality.

In summary, the proposed Valuation Model states an extended definition of the goal of conservation research: *the generation of knowledge that can be applied to achieve a maximum effective collection value through the optimization of the combination of preservation of and access to a collection as a whole, under a given conservation budget.* The extent to which this goal can be reached determines the success of that research. The *ex ante* estimation of the success of different research options offers an instrument for setting research priorities.

## Success of research

In the model presented, the valuation of research is linked to its effect, to the impact of a certain conservation measure connected with the research in question. The term 'measure' is used in this chapter as an umbrella for passive preservation measures, active conservation treatment methods and other conservation activities. Three scenarios can be distinguished according to the three different ways in which the knowledge generated by research may be implemented:

1    by introduction of new conservation measures
2    by improvement of already existing conservation measures
3    by cancellation of intended or existing conservation measures.

The introduction, improvement or cancellation of conservation measures will influence the effective collection value in both direct and indirect ways. The direct effect of a given measure can be defined as the change in effective collection value through a change in preservation and/or access directly associated with the measure itself. To quantify the direct change in effective collection value ($V_{dir}$) associated with a conservation measure ($m$), the initial values for preservation ($\Pi_i$) and access ($A_i$) and the new values ($\Pi_m$ and $A_m$) need to be estimated:

$$V_{dir} = \Pi_m \times A_m - \Pi_i \times A_i$$

In association with the introduction, improvement or cancellation of a specific measure there is, however, also the aspect of a reduction or an increase in the costs involved. From the assumption of a constant conservation budget, any increase or reduction in costs associated with a specific measure will lead to a shift within the total budget and thus a change in resources or costs used for all other conservation measures applied within an organization. Hence, such a shift in the conservation budget will affect preservation and access indirectly.

The indirect effect of a given conservation measure can now be defined as the change of the effective collection value through changes in preservation and access associated with *other* existing conservation measures due to a shift in the conservation budget. To quantify this indirect effect we have to know the mean efficiency ($\varepsilon$, epsilon) with which the total conservation budget ($B$) is utilized to maintain the current (initial) effective collection value ($V_i$).

$$\varepsilon = V_i / B$$

The indirect change of the effective collection value ($V_{ind}$) due to a pressure on the total conservation budget by the extra costs ($C_m$) involved with measure ($m$) can now be quantified as follows:

$$
\begin{aligned}
V_{ind} &= -C_m \times \varepsilon \\
&= -C_m \times (V_i / B) \\
&= -C_m \times (\Pi_i \times A_i)/B
\end{aligned}
$$

Note here the minus sign. If extra costs are involved with a measure ($m$), fewer funds will be available for the other existing conservation measures, which will have an indirect negative effect on the effective collection value. On the other hand, if a cost reduction can be realized for the measure, the value for the extra costs is negative, which implies that the indirect effect on the effective collection value will be positive.

The overall success ($S_m$) of a conservation research option, connected with a measure $m$, can now be expressed as the estimated net effect of that measure on the effective collection value:

$$S_m = V_{dir} + V_{ind}$$
$$= (\Pi_m \times A_m - \Pi_i \times A_i) - C_m \times (\Pi_i \times A_i)/B$$

This final 'formula of success' may appear pure theory. However, it unambiguously codifies and specifies our convictions formulated in the objective of paper conservation science, that is the generation of knowledge that can be applied to achieve a maximum effective collection value through optimization of the combination of preservation ($\Pi$) and access ($A$) of a collection as a whole, under a given conservation budget ($B$). In addition, this formula enables us to compare widely varying conservation research options in a single system, and enables objective decision making on research priorities.

## Discussion

The interpretation of the primary goal of conservation research as elaborated in the Valuation Model presented in this chapter has far-reaching consequences. The setting of research priorities according to this model is not only determined by the expected direct impact of research, but also by its estimated indirect, cost-related implications on the collection's preservation and access as a whole. The final choice for a certain research option is therefore strongly dependent on the position and policy of the respective collection-keeping institute. The introduction of a new conservation measure, including the costs involved, may improve the total cost-effectiveness for certain organizations, for example those having a large conservation budget, whereas for another institution, with a smaller budget, this same measure may lead to a reduction in cost-effectiveness. Although the incorporation of this kind of dependence in our Valuation Model certainly induces complications, it reflects the complex situation and kind of organizational differences that exist today.

The Valuation Model as an instrument to set conservation research priorities is principally based on the estimation of the 'success' of research options beforehand. These estimations should not be confused with the actual outcome of the research. It is not these estimations, but the results of the research itself and the conclusions that are drawn from these results that will be the sound basis of an adequate conservation policy. The estimated value of success only determines a 'ranking score' by which research priorities can be established in a well considered way. The eventual research results may prove or disprove the correctness of these estimations. Ultimately, the decision whether or not to implement the generated knowledge will determine the actual impact in practice.

Application of the Valuation Model necessitates that research proposals offer a clear insight into their expected contribution to the success indicators ('preservation', 'access', 'economy'). Of course, research options must be judged on normal scientific criteria as well. On the basis of all the characteristics of the Valuation Model, it is obvious that the use of this tool for setting conservation research priorities requires considerable insight and expertise regarding many different aspects of preservation and conservation. It is not intended to be a simple instrument to be used by anybody. The Valuation Model is an instrument that allows for responsible estimates of all parameters for prioritizing conservation research. It makes presentation and argumentation of choices transparent and verifiable.

In the joint paper conservation research programme in the Netherlands for the year 2005, the Valuation Model could not yet be fully applied. The concept of prioritizing conservation research by means of estimation and combination of its impact on the levels of preservation, access and economy is new and sufficient practical experience with the use of the Valuation Model still needs to be gained. The Valuation Model will be further discussed within the Dutch field of conservators, conservation scientists and collection managers. Experts from other research disciplines can also offer valuable comments: Professor Dr J. van der Pligt (University of Amsterdam Social Psychology Programme) is acknowledged for his recent suggestion to apply Multi-Attribute Utility Theory to aid the group decision-making process. This discussion will be important for the acceptance of the Valuation Model as a meaningful instrument for making future choices in our national, joint conservation research agenda. Research priorities and cost efficiency have been put forward as crucial issues by the international conservation science community. The setting of conservation research priorities and the importance of cost-effect analysis were on the agenda at international meetings in New York in 2003 and London in 2004 (see Bell et al., 2005). The Valuation Model described here is presented with the objective to offer a contribution in this area, and to invite the readers to participate in the discussion on its merits.

## Summary

In order to establish a coherent paper conservation research agenda, the setting of research priorities is necessary. For this purpose, the Valuation Model for Paper Conservation Research has been developed. Within the Valuation Model the 'ranking score' of the potential 'success' of conservation research is formulated in accordance with a stated definition of the goal of paper conservation research, that is the generation of knowledge to support the efficient use of resources in order to optimize the preservation of and access to our paper cultural heritage. Following this line of thought, three quantitative indicators for the 'success' of conservation research are distinguished: 'preservation', 'access' and 'economy'. The magnitudes of these indicators are estimated beforehand. For the mutual weighing and integration of the success indicators, the term 'effective collection value' is defined as the combination (product) of 'preservation' and 'access'. Within the concept of the Valuation Model, the success of conservation research is linked to the estimated impact of a conservation measure on the effective collection value. This impact is twofold: the direct effect of the conservation measure, and the indirect effect due to a shift in the total conservation budget created by the costs involved in that measure. With the final 'formula of success', the expected net effect on the effective collection value is calculated. In spite of its theoretical features, the Valuation Model for Paper Conservation Research presents a practical, straightforward elaboration of a principal statement on the objectives of conservation research, and offers a useful instrument enabling the necessary objectivity in decision making on research priorities. The merits of the Valuation Model still need to be further discussed and must be verified in practice.

## References

Bell, N., Knight, B. and Shenton, H. (2005) *Future Life of Collections, report on a meeting on Applied Conservation Research, held at the British Library on 27–28 September 2004, supported by the Andrew W. Mellon Foundation,* London, British Library.

Porck, H. J. and Teygeler, R. (2000) *Preservation Science Survey: an overview of recent developments in research on the conservation of selected analog library and archival materials,* Washington DC, Council on Library and Information Resources.

Rosvall, J., Engelbrektsson, N., Lagerqvist, B. and van Gigch, J. P. (1995) *International Perspectives on Strategic Planning for Research and Education in Conservation. Presented at: Convegno internazionale di studi 'Giovanni Secco Suardo. La cultura del restauro tra tutela e conservazione dell' opere d'arte',* Bergamo, 9–11 March.

Waller, Robert R. (2003) *Cultural Property Risk Analysis Model: development and application to preventive conservation at the Canadian Museum of Nature,* Göteborg Studies in Conservation 13, Acta Universitatis Gothoburgensis, Göteborg, Göteborg University.

# CHAPTER 7

# Preservation of audiovisual media: traditional to interactive formats

Bob Pymm

## Introduction

At their 27th Annual Conference, FIAT (2004), the International Federation of Television Archives, formalized an International Appeal for the Preservation of the World's Audiovisual Heritage. In this appeal they called attention to the critically endangered state of much of the world's audiovisual heritage, particularly in less advanced countries, and issued a call for action to professionals everywhere to press for more resources and attention to be paid to this task. With the growing acceptance that audiovisual materials form an essential component of the collective memory for the last 100 years or so, and that the pace of deterioration and technological obsolescence makes it increasingly likely that a large proportion of these items has already been lost forever, this call for action was intended to mobilize all those involved in cultural preservation to lobby for the necessary human and financial resources to give the task the priority it deserved.

For libraries, archives and museums who have a tradition of acquiring the range of audiovisual media on a wide variety of physical formats, this call to action confirms what they already know: that there are problems with preserving and accessing older formats and that the scale of the problem is, in many organizations, daunting. The large collections of photographs, film and audiotape that have been established, together with the less common collections of discs and videotape, are demanding attention now. And while these physical collections pose significant challenges, the new digital formats have added another level of complexity to the preservation issue that calls for 'new ways of thinking about preservation, and new skills' (Harvey, 2004, 1).

Much has been written about the long-term management of the physical media and this chapter will provide a broad overview of preservation practices that most institutions, lacking highly specific and dedicated resources for audiovisual preservation, can adopt in order to prolong the life of this material. For the emerging digital objects and their preservation needs, the situation is less clear and discussion will centre upon broad approaches to dealing with these new collections.

However, prolonging the life of physical or digital objects is only one part of the complex preservation equation. Another major factor comprises the availability of playback equipment (mechanical or computer) upon which most audiovisual media depend. While photographs - and, to some degree, film - can be accessed using simple or no playback mechanisms, most of the other formats require sophisticated, purpose-designed machines or hardware/software to do the task. Without these in good working order, accessing the information on the original audiovisual carrier may not be possible. For traditional formats, Boston (2003) has noted that the increasing obsolescence of the machines needed for playback has been a major driver in the uptake of digitization programmes in sound archives, and Edmondson (2004) raises the issue of the problem faced by collecting institutions having to maintain obsolete technology which has been abandoned by industry.

Thus, the traditional preservation approach has been to ensure the availability of appropriate equipment, as well as maintaining the carrier in good condition, in order to provide long-term access to an item. And while this may still be a very necessary approach for many, the advent of digital capture and replay has changed the scenario markedly. Indeed, the production of physical audiovisual carriers will decline significantly over the coming years as more and more material is made available as computer files and not in any physical form. A recent OECD report (2005) noted a 20% fall in the global sales of CDs between 1999 and 2003, and while it could not prove a causal relationship between the availability of online content and this drop, it does suggest that 2004 can be seen as a turning point in the availability, and popularity, of the online marketing of music. Given this growth, for institutions acquiring such digital files, whether they comprise audio or visual information, the practices and procedures involved in their preservation will be little different from those involved with the preservation of digital text files. The differences in approach between the preservation of printed materials, and the preservation of audiovisual materials that have existed for 100 years or more, will no longer be relevant.

## The traditional media

Preservation activity in cultural institutions can be seen as comprising two distinct approaches: passive and active. *Passive* preservation refers to the correct storage and packaging of collection material that helps to slow down or even halt deterioration. This approach will not make anything 'better' but does buy time and enable prioritizing to be undertaken in a systematic, less pressured environment. This prioritizing is necessary in order to identify individual items that may require *active* conservation treatment and to queue them to an appropriate facility according to their needs. This is very much a hands-on approach, where an item gets in-depth attention. For most institutions, resources are not usually available to undertake active preservation at anything other than a modest level.

The issue of prioritization is an important one calling for a clear policy and commitment from management. Lindner talks about using the hospital triage approach: separating out problem items, applying priorities and 'saving what you can, while you can, at a reasonable cost and a reasonable timeframe' (2005, 2). By prioritizing certain items ahead of others, an organization is effectively making decisions that may mean the eventual loss of some material. Thus the rationale behind the prioritization needs to be clear-cut and publicly defensible with the policy readily accessible to any enquirer; for an example of this see the Bibliothèque Nationale de France's criteria for prioritizing digitization of their sound collection (Carou, 2002).

The criteria used for prioritization will vary between collecting institutions, but will probably include a combination of:

- legal responsibility (the institution is legislated to acquire and preserve such material, e.g., national archives)
- rarity (is this the only copy known to have survived or are others held in-house or in other institutions?)
- significance (is this an outstanding example of its genre, e.g. for technical innovation, popularity, award winning, etc.?)
- deterioration (the physical item is in very poor condition and likely to be lost unless something is done)
- obsolescence (the format is no longer supported, playback equipment is hard to find and maintain and staff with the necessary skill base to work with the equipment are difficult to find), and
- access demand (are the titles in demand by users?).

Like other areas to do with preserving collections, there is generally no 'right' answer that will fit all situations. Every organization will have to balance the needs of the collections, the demands of its users and the resources it possesses in determining preservation activity. In addition, with digital collections there are other factors, such as technology and its continual evolution, which will also impact upon preservation practices and the costs and effort involved. These generally will make the long-term preservation process of digital materials more complex but, on the positive side, will be less resource-intensive and should lead to a greater percentage of the collection being fully preserved at any one time. For the physical collection, given the resource-intensive nature of the preservation task, passive preservation becomes the key to the survival of the bulk of the collection.

### Physical storage

The concept of passive preservation is based upon proper preparation, packaging and storage of material. Thus it is not really passive, but a proactive approach to deal in the best way possible with large amounts of materials given limited budgets. For organizations with significant collections, basic storage principles are the key to their long-term stability.

Before any collection item is placed into storage it needs to be examined and if necessary some basic treatment applied, such as cleaning or rewinding. Care needs to be taken to ensure problems such as mould or vinegar syndrome are properly identified at this stage in order to ensure appropriate actions are taken. Storing deteriorating materials such as these in the main run with the rest of the collection may cause problems through contamination. Mould is a common problem in areas of high humidity and if clearly visible, the item needs to be cleaned under controlled conditions; there are real occupational health and safety issues involved in dealing with mould, and obtaining professional advice is recommended.

Some form of catalogue entry needs to be updated with this information, particularly if there are signs of deterioration. This is important in order to assess the speed or nature of deterioration if an item is examined again in say ten years' time. While entering condition details to the catalogue, it may be that the item's priority for treatment or copying is assessed and this information recorded. An item then needs to be labelled appropriately, taking care not to interfere with the object itself, and placed in appropriate packaging.

If the item is likely to stay in this packaging for the coming years, then care should be taken in selecting the packaging material. Some general points are that packaging is better if made from inert materials such as polypropylene, rather than organic matter such as cardboard; that acid free paper be used for bags, inserts or dividers; that items are not jammed into containers but fit comfortably; and for reels of film, that they are loosely wound on to cores or reels for long-term storage. For collections of acetate film (both still and moving image) or tape, a condition known as vinegar syndrome has received a lot of attention in recent years. Its name is due to the readily identifiable smell given off by the chemical decomposition of the film. Given the long-term problems this can cause – and its ability to spread through collections – small absorbent packets called molecular sieves are sometimes stored with film collections that are at risk. These packets can be placed inside film cans or in drawers of negatives in order to absorb the decomposition products, slowing the rate of decomposition. They should be replaced at regular intervals (National Film and Sound Archive, 2003a). Ideally, affected materials should be stored separately from the main collection to avoid any risk of contamination.

If possible, both the item itself, and its packaging, should be appropriately labelled. This will not always be possible owing to the nature of the item but when it is done, it provides added security to ensure an item can be readily identified if it becomes separated from its container. Once properly packaged, items will generally be shelved. Films stored in cans should be shelved in small stacks, one on top of the other, rather than vertically on the shelf. Other audiovisual media such as tapes and discs can be stored vertically. Small items, such as photographs, audio cassettes, DATs etc., are best stored in archival 'shoe boxes' made from polypropylene or acid free card. These provide a cheap, easy and very practical storage option for smaller items that can otherwise be difficult to control on large shelves.

The three major factors comprising good storage for virtually all audiovisual materials are cool temperatures, moderate to low relative humidity and stable conditions. A number of standards have been developed and recommendations made, particularly relating to film. Both FIAF (the International Federation of Film Archives) and the American National Standards Institute (ANSI) have produced guidelines covering long-term storage of film. This has generated a significant level of debate and discussion as to various film types, the most appropriate conditions for long-term preservation, and what is actually meant by *permanent* preservation. In addition, there are international standards for the storage of CDs and other optical media for the long term.

All of these standards are based on the principle that if material is stored under these conditions, it should not deteriorate noticeably over a period of a 100 or more years. This may be true, and a CD may very well survive in a pristine condition for the next century, but will a CD player be available in the year 2100? Storage conditions are important, but to reiterate, they are just one piece in the complex preservation puzzle.

For still or moving image film, cool temperatures (around 16°C) with a relative humidity of 35% provide the best conditions. For colour film in particular, temperatures below freezing (from -5 to -18°C) provide the best environment to limit dye fade. However, apart from the difficulty of creating these conditions, the issue of accessing such material and the need for gradual acclimatization makes this ideal scenario difficult for most non-specialist organizations to achieve in practice (National Film and Sound Archive, 2003b).

For magnetic tapes and discs of varying types, cool (18–24°C) conditions and a similar or slightly higher relative humidity are recommended (National Film and Sound Archive, 2003b). For most organizations, temperature control can be managed relatively easily. Humidity control is far more difficult and, depending upon the external environment and the design of the storage facility, may require a considerable investment in appropriate equipment.

Maintaining stability in the running of storage environments is probably as important as creating the right temperature and humidity. In a wide-ranging paper prepared by the UNESCO Memory of the World Committee covering all aspects of the preservation of the documentary heritage (in all formats), the Committee emphasizes the basic requirement of a stable temperature and stable humidity levels (UNESCO, c.2000).

The design of any storage facility, be it an entire purpose-built building or just a small room, will have a big impact on storage conditions. Small spaces are generally easier to condition than large ones (but ultimately less efficient than conditioning large areas due to the larger surface area to volume ratio in small spaces), walls should be insulated if possible and, ideally, entry should be through a double door system through an air lock. There should be no windows and lighting should be automatic so that it switches off when no one is in the area. While compactus shelving makes best use of space, air flow is important, so ensure that the design and installation of compactus takes into account the necessary movement of air. Good air flow will help minimize the potential for mould growth – probably the major risk faced by audiovisual collections – should humidity levels get too high. Newnham and Garvie (2005) reported that the result of several weeks' high humidity in a film storage area led to significant damage in the form of mould growth and ferrotyping requiring considerable conservation effort to recover the damaged items.

Fire suppressant systems are a vexed question for cultural institutions. Sprinkler systems are used but have obvious drawbacks and gas systems are very expensive. Each institution will have to decide what it feels is best for its own situation but, regardless of the approach, Ling (1999, 56) recommends that smoke and heat detectors should be located throughout the facility, connected to a central control panel.

Finally, air-conditioning should provide air cleaning and filtration at a high level in order to remove dust particles and chemicals as far as possible.

## Monitoring

Having established the best storage conditions that resources allow, it is necessary to ensure that both the facility itself, and the collection within it, are regularly monitored. Like any large collection that is only accessed irregularly, some form of cyclical maintenance or risk management procedures need to be set in place to ensure that the storage facility is performing as anticipated and that the collection is stable.

Monitoring conditions within the store can be done using fairly basic or far more sophisticated tools. Traditionally, maximum and minimum thermometers and a sling psychrometer were used to monitor temperature and relative humidity. This basic equipment is still available and modestly priced but does need to be regularly calibrated in order to maintain its accuracy. Most institutions have moved to using digital monitoring and recording devices which monitor conditions at set intervals, can be programmed to raise alarms if things go wrong and can be linked to an existing computer network to enable data to be downloaded and conditions checked without actually entering the store. With this level of monitoring there should be no likelihood of any prolonged breakdown of conditions passing unnoticed.

Monitoring of the collection itself in storage will be a far more time consuming and less automated process. Usually, it will be impossible to examine every item in store on a regular basis (the ideal situation). Instead, some form of sampling has to be undertaken with the results from the sample extrapolated to apply to the entire collection. For this sample to provide an accurate reflection of the condition of the entire collection, it needs to be carefully selected. There are a number of statistical techniques available to ensure this but, in general, care must be taken to ensure that the samples come from a population with common characteristics. These characteristics may include storage location (e.g., the same vault, the same compactus); material composition (e.g., the same brand of audiotape); material type (e.g., 35 mm colour transparencies, audio cassettes); chronology (e.g., all pre-1914 photographs), etc.

Depending upon material type, condition checking of the sample may require visual inspection for conditions such as mould, buckling, scratches, etc., as well as some form of testing (from simple to sophisticated) to identify deterioration such as vinegar syndrome in acetate film, the level of dye fade in a colour transparency, the loss of signal from a particular brand of audiotape or 'sticky shed' syndrome on videotape. Some of these tests can be performed with limited equipment or training while others may require a level of sophistication where it will be necessary to bring in outside expertise.

As part of this condition inspection, for materials such as audio or videotape, it has been generally recommended that periodic rewinding – and, if equipment is available, cleaning, of the tape – will help even out the tension and physical stresses in the tape itself. However, there is some disagreement over the merits of this, and care must be taken to use professional equipment and trained personnel (Lindner, c.2000).

The results from any monitoring must be carefully recorded against the catalogue record for the object so that, when the condition survey is undertaken again, comparisons can be made as to any noticeable deterioration or damage that has occurred during the intervening period. The monitoring process may also highlight items that are in need of treatment. These should then be prioritized and placed in an active preservation queue.

## Active preservation: copying

The traditional method for ensuring the long-term survival of audiovisual materials has been copying from one physical format to another. This provides additional copies of the item, often on better quality formats than originally acquired, and provides the opportunity for conservation work to be performed at the same time. In undertaking this work, Wheeler's (1994) advice from a decade ago remains just as relevant today: 'choose a format that is popular ... and buy the best quality equipment available'. Aim for something that is in wide use and likely to have the relevant equipment available into the foreseeable future. While Wheeler was referring to the analogue world of tape machines and equipment, his advice is just as valid to the digital world of hardware and software, to be discussed later.

Of course, an item has to be in a physical state that makes copying possible. Films that have damaged sprockets, excessive scratching, broken splices, etc., will have to be prepared for any copying process, and for magnetic tapes care must be taken to ensure they are not suffering from stickiness or shedding which may mean the item is unplayable or will require sophisticated treatment before it can be run through a player. Any of this conservation work requires high levels of staff expertise and equipment, and for most institutions, the work will need to be outsourced to specialist organizations.

Copying is an expensive – and for a medium such as film, complex – option that for many institutions can only be undertaken on a relatively small scale. In a wide-ranging review of acetate film preservation in Australia, the National Library noted the resource-intensive nature of copying projects and raised the issue of quality control and technical standards that need to be applied in any copying proposal. The appendix to their report provides a good overview of the costs associated with a range of preservation activities for audiovisual media and provides a useful guideline for assessing various approaches (National Library of Australia, 2000). The report also quotes Steve Puglia, who conducted a comparison of the costs involved in undertaking an analogue copying programme for photographic materials against the provision of good quality storage. His findings that storage is considerably less expensive than duplication confirms that such copying, for most organizations, will always be limited to their priority material (ibid., 2000, 34). In the short period since these findings were published, however, preservation copying of photographic stills has virtually ceased, with digital duplication becoming the primary preservation route with one of its advantages being its cost-effectiveness.

For analogue materials, copying will also pose the problem of the copy being a somewhat inferior version of the original. For film this is less of an issue as very high-quality copies can be produced, but for tape it is a much more serious consideration. Generational loss is far higher with analogue copying of tapes and then there is the question of how long will the new format be supported before it too becomes obsolete? For many archives, the use of an analogue video format, Betacam SP, for preservation copies was standard practice during the 1990s, yet in 2001 Sony announced they would no longer be making Betacam SP machines although they will continue to support the format for the next few years (AMIA, 2004). Thus what was once seen as a good archival medium for video preservation has now created another collection of obsolete formats that will have to be transferred to something else if they are to be accessible in 20 years' time.

## Active preservation: digitizing

Starting with photographs and other documentary material, digitization has now become the standard approach to 'copying' paper or photographic collections; it is commonly used for copying audio materials and is increasingly being adopted for moving image items. This rapid uptake of digital technologies has called for new policies to be developed, for technical standards to be established and for an increasing reliance upon IT and its technical infrastructure. However, Harvey (2004) notes that from his interviews with those working in the field, technical issues did not rate highly as a major area of concern. Rather, the place of digital preservation in the broader institutional context was seen as needing further emphasis. In addition, Edmondson (2004) raises the aesthetic and ethical issues involved in transferring analogue materials to digital, and questions whether the resultant digital object can ever be a true substitute for the original item, providing the viewer or listener with the same experience. This is a valid concern, with digitization usually being primarily concerned with capturing what the archive community describe as the 'essence' of an item – its essential information content – rather than necessarily creating a totally faithful reproduction of the analogue original. This then raises the issue of what happens with the analogue item once it has been digitized. Generally, at the very least, the best copy of the original analogue item should be preserved in order to overcome these concerns and also to provide the best possible medium for any future digitization activity that may be undertaken (e.g., if more sophisticated technologies become available).

For audiovisual collections, digitization offers much but also requires a lot. While digitizing photographs or other two-dimensional documents is straightforward, with well defined standards, relatively low-cost equipment, and a skills base that is becoming more and more widely available, the same cannot be said of sound or moving image digitization: for extensive discussion of still image digitization refer to the TASI (Technical Advisory Service for Images) website at www.tasi.ac.uk/newsarchive.html. Despite this added complexity, and the costs involved, digitization of existing audio and videotape collections has become a necessity if the information stored on these tapes is to remain accessible. Manufacturers have ceased producing most of the appropriate playback equipment for analogue audio and video and will wind down support of existing equipment over the coming few years. Even the tapes themselves are difficult to source and will soon no longer be manufactured. The technology is forcing change, whether we like it or not.

For audio or video digitization, issues to be considered include:

- the selection of the best copy and the level of preparation: condition checking, conservation or cleaning required
- the amount of space required for the resultant files (e.g. an hour of uncompressed video may take as much as 140 gigabytes of disk space) (Cohen and Rosenzweig, c.2002)
- the need for high-quality playback equipment and experienced personnel to work with the original formats in order to minimize problems, such as signal dropout with video or audiotape, to ensure the best possible digital product
- the necessary equipment – hardware and software – to undertake the conversion process
- whether clean-up or editing of the file will be undertaken (e.g., removing clicks and hiss from audio recordings). There are different views on the desirability of this (it depends upon the objectives of your organization), as well as practical considerations over the time and effort required
- the level of expertise available to ensure the quality of the digital conversion

- standards for the digital capture (e.g. for sound, a sampling rate of 96 kHz with a bit depth of 24 bits is a current high-end standard but this may change as technologies improve). For long-term preservation, capture and storage in an uncompressed form (resulting in larger files) is preferable. For audio, common capture formats are WAVE (.wav) or, of similar quality but using a 'lossy' compression algorithm, MP3 files, which use less space and are thus quicker to download. For video, MPEG-2 provides DVD-like quality, and a relatively new standard, Motion JPEG2000 (MJ2), has seen rapid uptake in the library and archive world due to its open standard and lossless compression mode. Pearson and Gill (2005) conclude that MJ2 has promise as an archival format but that more time is needed to evaluate its practical implementation. In addition, more compressed formats, such as QuickTime, allow for smaller files and again download more quickly, but are not seen as appropriate as a preservation standard.

Digitizing film will generally be a costly procedure, requiring the work to be outsourced to a specialist in the field. However, if a loss of quality is acceptable, it is possible to establish an in-house facility at modest cost where the film is captured on video and subsequently digitized. Due to the size of the digitized versions, it is common practice to create copies on digital tape rather than relying on computer files. This makes the digital copy near-line, rather than online, and it may be useful to select from the digital copy sample grabs from the full production to place online.

Digitizing video can be undertaken in-house given a modest investment in equipment. Like film, the output will generally be to digital tape rather than a computer file, although this may change over time as technologies improve and storage costs fall. One of the major challenges with video is the sheer volume of material and the number of formats held by many institutions. This inevitably means prioritizing and the possibility that the standards used for the digital copy may be less than the ideal given the resources available.

Digitizing audio is more straightforward and can be done by simply attaching the playback equipment to a PC equipped with the appropriate sound capture card and software. However, for preservation purposes, using as high a quality as possible standalone ADC (analogue to digital converter) is preferable. The International Association of Sound and Audiovisual Archives (Bradley, 2004) provides detailed specifications for converters and related sound cards and the file formats recommended for audio digitization. Being significantly smaller than moving image files, audio files will usually be held on a local file server.

An integral component of the digitization process is ensuring that appropriate documentation is maintained relating to the creation of the digital object. As well as technical information regarding formats, software and security, there are provenance issues related to the evolution of the object from its original form and ownership issues dealing with rights and restrictions. If digitized copies are to be made available in the online environment, then it is essential to ensure any necessary clearances and approvals are obtained from rights holders before the material is made available and any limitations on access clearly delineated. Secondly, the digital files need to be secure, with access properly controlled. Back-ups and preservation copies may be held on separate systems and all access to files can be logged for security purposes.

## Digital broadcast materials

With the gradual demise of analogue formats, libraries and archives are increasingly faced with the problem of how to acquire material that traditionally came on a physical carrier such as a disc or videotape but now only exists as a computer file. This raises questions to do with acquisitions and collection management, as well as the ongoing preservation and accessibility of these new digital objects.

Broadcast materials may be acquired in the more traditional manner (e.g., downloaded onto a medium such as DVD), e-mailed as an attached file or captured directly from the broadcast itself. Given a modest investment in hardware and software, and once the relevant permissions have been obtained, the actual acquisition process is fairly straightforward and for direct capture can be automated to a large degree. Pymm and Kaeding (2004), in their discussion of the satellite capture of radio broadcasts, note that, once established, it is easy, and tempting, to download more material than can then be satisfactorily described and catalogued. This is something that has to be carefully managed to ensure that the materials that are acquired are properly accessioned and retrievable.

For television broadcasts the issue of quality arises. While the capture of the broadcast may be straightforward, the question of what is actually being captured and retained needs to be carefully considered. To a large degree this again depends upon the objectives of the organization. If programmes are being acquired to provide access only, then the broadcast format as captured will be quite acceptable. However, if the programme is being acquired with a view to long-term preservation and possible repackaging or repurposing, then it may be that the file captured from the broadcast will be of insufficient quality. In an ideal world, the preservation copy would be a direct copy of the broadcast programme taken from the broadcaster's file servers - not necessarily an easy thing to organize and certainly not as straightforward as an automated broadcast capture process.

For web broadcasts, and particularly interactive programmes, new challenges arise. The dynamic nature of these productions makes the capture and preservation of such programmes in the traditional manner (as finished products) more difficult. If we cannot stabilize the object or draw clear boundaries around it due to its external links, then what criteria can be used to determine what or how much is captured and when? The issue of authenticity (what did the producer actually intend?) has also been noted by de Jong (2002) as another problem that does not have a clear-cut solution in this environment. Thus institutions are having to develop new policies and approaches, as well as technological solutions, to handle this new form of programming which will inevitably grow in importance over the coming years.

Preserving digital objects that come as physical items, such as DVDs, will require the same approach as the more traditional formats: good storage, a player and a strategy for migration to another format at a later date once the current technology becomes problematic. For items that are already in a digital format (such as CDs or DVDs), the migration route will be simpler than for moving analogue items to digital. But it does provide a workload issue as large numbers will need to follow the migration path.

For items received as files, the issues related to audiovisual productions are much the same as for any other computer file with the major concern being compatibility – does the collecting institution have the appropriate software to access and play back the file? Given the wide variety of possible file formats and plug-ins, it is essential that files are checked at the time of acquisition to ensure their usability and make it possible to undertake a longer-term preservation strategy for the item. For large files, it may also be necessary to try to 'chunk' or modularize the file to make it easier to handle.

## Digital preservation

For any digital object there is the very real issue of ensuring its long-term accessibility and the more complex the digital object (as in audio or video items or web pages), the more demanding this process will be. Yet it has to be done, with digital formats having, for archival purposes, incredibly short life-spans. A fuller discussion of this topic appears in Chapter 8, but there are some specific concerns relevant to audiovisual collections. These relate mainly to file formats and proprietary software that make migration to new systems more demanding. This may result in the 'look and feel' of the original being changed, even though the content is preserved. Whether this is an issue or not depends upon the organization and its aims. As Deegan and Tanner (2002, 199) note:

> Pursuing a goal of absolute fidelity to originals can be a counter-cultural anachronism that does not reflect what happens in the analogue world. The ordinary reader of Shakespeare for instance, does not usually access the text through the 16th century versions, but through modern editions.

A recent example that effectively illustrates these and other issues was the effort required to migrate the BBC's Domesday Book Project from 1986. With the original versions from 1086 still well preserved and available, the irony of the near loss of the 1986 version is evident. Briefly, the BBC commissioned the new Domesday Book to celebrate 900 years of the original. Using the then latest technology of videodiscs (holding a mixture of analogue and digital information) plus a BBC microcomputer and purpose-built software, this new survey of the UK was made available to schools, libraries and universities throughout the country at the end of 1986. Fortunately, a complete copy (hardware, software and data) was placed in the National Archives (Public Record Office at the time). In 2002, staff at the National Archives were concerned over the long-term accessibility of this data and started a full preservation process to migrate the information to a format more easily maintained into the future. This raised interesting issues. Was the 'look and feel' of the original to be maintained or, with the current state of technology, should the analogue images in particular be preserved at an improved standard? After considerable discussion it was agreed that the highest quality approach would be taken, with the result that it would not be a direct emulation of the original 1986 version. Reverse engineering the proprietary software proved a major challenge but fortunately one of the writers involved with the original programming was still available to assist in the process. The migration of this one, admittedly specialized product, took 16 months and a huge investment of resources (Darlington et al., 2003).

The Domesday Project sends a very clear signal of the complexity of the migration process if the original objects are not created with long-term preservation in mind. It illustrates clearly the necessity for creating digital objects using commonly supported and documented standards, the maintenance of good records describing the object and its creation and provenance, and the need to undertake migration or other preservation strategies within time frames that are disturbingly short for most institutions.

To conclude, Edmondson (2004, 20) makes the very clear point that 'nothing has ever been preserved – at best, it is being preserved'. He goes on to emphasize that this points to preservation being a never-ending management process, not a one-off task. And while it may be that technological development, particularly in the areas of emulation, will mitigate this process for digital objects, preservation will remain a major, resource-intensive task for all of the 'memory' institutions.

## References

AMIA Association of Moving Image Archivists (2004) *Reformatting for Preservation: understanding tape formats and other conversion issues,* www.amianet.org/publication/resources/guidelines/videofacts/reformatting. html [accessed 1 July 2005].

Boston, G. (2003) *Survey of Endangered Audiovisual Carriers*, Paris, UNESCO, http://portal.unesco.org/ci/en/file_download.php/ dfb2ad0ec5e386a5040cf35fc58f029bSurvey+Report.pdf [accessed 20 June 2005].

Bradley, K. (ed.) (2004) *Guidelines on the Production and Preservation of Digital Audio Objects (IASA-TC04)*, Aarhus, International Association of Sound and Audiovisual Archives.

Carou, A. (2002) Digitization and Digital Asset Preservation at the Bibliothèque Nationale de France, *IASA Journal*, **20** (2), www.iasa-web.org/journal_articles/carou_alain.pdf [accessed 22 June 2005].

Cohen, D. J. and Rosenzweig, R. (c.2002) *Digital History: a guide to gathering, preserving and presenting the past on the web*, Philadelphia, PA, University of Pennsylvania Press, http://chnm.gmu.edu/digitalhistory/ [accessed 14 July 2005].

Darlington, J., Finney, A. and Pearce, A. (2003) Domesday Redux: the rescue of the BBC Domesday project videodiscs, *Ariadne*, Issue 36, www.ariadne.ac.uk/issue36/tna/ [accessed 13 July 2005].

Deegan, M. and Tanner, S. (2002) *Digital Futures: strategies for the information age*, London, Library Association Publishing.

Edmondson, R. (2004) *Audiovisual Archiving: philosophy and principles*, Paris, UNESCO, http://portal.unesco.org/ci/en/ev.php-URL_ID=15592&URL_DO= DO_TOPIC&URL_SECTION=201.html [accessed 22 June 2005].

Harvey, R. (2004) *The Preservation of Digital Documentary Heritage: lessons from Australian experience, paper presented at the Made in Aotearoa: learn, network, celebrate LIANZA Conference, Auckland*, Library and Information Association of Aotearoa New Zealand, www.lianza.org.nz/events/conference2004/papers/harvey.pdf [accessed 1 July 2005].

International Federation of Television Archives (2004) *International Appeal for the Preservation of the Audiovisual Heritage*, www.fiatifta.org/aboutfiat/policy/petition/index.php [accessed 30 June 2005].

de Jong, A. (2002) *Preservation of the Web: issues for audiovisual archives, paper*

# CHAPTER 8

# Challenges of managing the digitally born artefact

Barbara Reed

## Introduction

This chapter examines the challenges of managing digitally born artefacts. It raises more questions and issues than provides answers. A large body of international research is being undertaken both within and across information disciplines in digital preservation. A growing body of practical experience is emerging. At this time the conclusions are that no one 'solution' exists to the challenges in digital preservation and that multiple strategies should be pursued with equal vigour. This conclusion is not intended to encourage information professionals to adopt a wait and see strategy, for digital resources are fragile, vulnerable and in need of constant attention in order to exist in both the short term and long term. No cultural heritage institution can afford to postpone the challenges of managing the digitally born artefact.

## Why are digitally born artefacts different?

Chapter 4 has addressed issues of surrogacy and the artefact. This chapter is dealing with those artefacts whose initial and continuing manifestation is as a digital resource, rather than those whose format was altered to a digital manifestation. There is a cross-over relationship between these two broad categories of resource. Once something has been rendered digital, the preservation challenges to maintain that object in its new form coincide with the challenges of the digitally born. However, the challenges are simpler. Not only is there the potential safeguard that the artefact may exist in its original format, but by implication the artefact reformatted will already exist in a controlled environment and have been subject to the controls of a formal institution (Lynch, 2004, 610). No such safeguards, real or implicit, can be assumed to exist for the mass of digitally born material.

The vast majority of original information being produced is in digital format. Estimates of quantity in 2003 indicate five exabytes (or $10^{18}$ bytes) of new information was produced in 2002, with over 92% of this stored on magnetic media, primarily hard disk. This represents a growth of about 30% per year between 1999 and 2002. The largest area of growth is in the area of office documents. The world wide web is estimated to contain 167 terabytes of information on the surface web with more than 400 times this amount on the deep web (that part of the web driven by databases that create web pages on demand (OCLC, 2004). The technology has made every organization and many individuals 'accidental' publishers. The huge volume and diverse sources of digital information make the issues of identifying and working out preservation strategies for the information of long-term importance created by our society staggeringly difficult to contemplate. Just what should we be trying to preserve?

Digitally born resources have with them immediate and omnipresent issues with the format and media on which they are stored. These challenges exist at a number of layers. First, there is the software program in which the information is written. Rules of thumb suggest that software programs will have a generational life of about five years. Beyond that, documents created in original software may be read in other software, or may need to be converted or migrated into forms compatible with newer software. The software itself is usually written to work on specific types of operating systems (e.g., Windows XP or Apple, etc.). These operating systems, too, are subject to change over quite short periods of time. The operating systems may also have a hardware dependency – they only operate on specific types of computer or generations of hardware. Then there is the media on which the information is preserved – hard disks, magnetic tape, floppy disks, flash disks, etc. Each of these media has quite rapid cycles of obsolescence. Without attention to each of these technical dependencies throughout the existence of the resource, it will not survive to be available as cultural heritage in the long term.

These technological dependencies and obsolescence issues are perhaps the most easily recognized of the challenges to digital preservation as they are confrontational, unquestionably omnipresent, and many practitioners have experienced them on an individual basis in dealing with their own personal records. As the following stories show, our community has been concerned about this aspect for over 15 years. One of the best known examples is that of the BBC Domesday Project, a huge multimedia project undertaken in the UK in 1986 to celebrate the 900th anniversary of the original Domesday Book. The project involved school children across the UK contributing images and video of locations, written pieces on specific localities, statistics and virtual tours. The project was compiled on to two 12-inch video discs, which were written in a language called BCPL and ran on BBC microcomputers, widely deployed in UK schools in the 1980s. By 2002 the program, the hardware and the media were unreadable except in a few rare instances where the original machine survived. The irony, of course, is that the original Domesday Book is perfectly accessible over 900 years later (CAMiLEON Project, 2002).

In the USA, the 1960 census data was written on to tapes able to be accessed by the Univac1, a technology that has now been obsolete for nearly three decades. This was widely cited as an instance of neglect, bringing about the virtual destruction of the information as it was unreadable. In fact, as the subsequent clarification of the story makes clear, there was no expectation that the specific data on these tapes would be preserved for the long term (Adams and Brown, 2000), and therefore no preservation strategies had been deployed. Similar stories have occurred in Australia, where petroleum data tapes of considerable commercial value from the 1960s were only readable on two machines in the world – one located in Texas and one in Japan (Stuckey, 1991).

Obsolescence and volume are just two of the distinguishing features of digital resources. A more basic and challenging notion is that of conceptualizing a digital resource. In the longish period of transition between paper-based forms and digital forms, it is inevitable that we wish to draw analogies to what we are familiar with. In decades past we might console ourselves that if a digital document was important, we could print it out – render it into a paper format. But as soon as we moved away from the generation of technology that were effectively typewriter replacements, the nature of digital documents has never really permitted that clean a comparison to paper. The technology enables documents to have links embedded, sourcing values from other documents, spreadsheets, images, etc. Documents seen on web pages often never exist independently as documents, being created 'on the fly' by databases and tailored to user preferences and profiles. What I might see may be quite different from what you might see. It is difficult in this world to separate the act of creating the document from the act of viewing the document, which actually brings the various components together on a specific viewing device. Even if we limit our considerations to the familiar office-type documents, these contain a myriad of unseen links and metadata associated with the production process itself. The paper rendition of a digital resource is not a complete representation of that resource – it represents a selection, or, with embedded links, a point-in-time representation of that dynamic document. The notion of document in the digital world has always been dubious, hence the Dublin Core community's very early focus on 'document-like objects'.

Many digital resources just cannot be rendered to paper, and as the digital environment moves to a greater integration of multimedia, this once automatic association with what we know as paper documents is receding quickly. For the cultural heritage community, future access is a major driver for all our preservation activities, and with this in mind, the strategy of print to paper will not serve our increasingly digitally focused clientele, even if it were a good technical solution, or one that was achievable for the huge quantity of material.

The metaphors and analogies that we inevitably draw to the paper world need to be reconsidered. While linking to the familiar is a necessary transitional step, considering and treating digital resources as if they were the traditional physical resources with which we have so much accumulated experience, is likely to be a significant block to being able to move into the digital world. Significantly different methods are needed to identify, manage and access dynamic digital resources.

## Conceptual challenges of the digital resource

As a part of reconceptualizing what digital resources are, a number of concepts need to be revisited. One of the most challenging is rethinking what a digital object is, its boundaries and the responsibilities associated with it. Our prevailing notions of preservation practice are based on the assumption of physical possession of an object. Similarly, they are predicated on assumptions about the value of the originals. These two issues are substantially challenged in the digital world.

Physical ownership of digital resources is no longer a given for cultural heritage organizations in the digital world. One of the clearest examples of this is in the subscription or licensing models operating within libraries for electronic journals. Here subscription is for access, divorced from possession, a distinction which has caused considerable anxiety for academics seeking access to e-journals to which their library has ceased subscriptions. It was there once, but the models of subscription have removed the capacity to access it once the licence expires or was terminated (e.g., see ABC Radio, 2001). Therefore, while superficially similar to print, the 'ownership' is actually completely different. The ownership is retained by the publisher.

But does the publisher have the associated responsibilities for long-term preservation and access that a library traditionally adopted for resources brought within its institutional hold? In a world where many institutions and individuals are 'accidental publishers', can we assume that responsibility for ownership involves a responsibility for long-term access? If a third-party institution, such as a library, archive or museum, actually takes physical possession of a digital resource, does this imply that they will undertake the perpetual preservation of that resource? Can concepts such as copyright be stretched to include the responsibility to ensure that resources will be preserved? If the preservation rights are assumed, does this include the right to mandate access controls? If left with bodies other than public institutions, will the public right to access be protected? Digital rights and the increasingly sophisticated understanding that multiple responsibilities and rights exist within the previous paper-based assumptions of ownership are beginning to change. What is clear is that the relationships and responsibilities associated with maintaining and preserving the object and access to the object over time can no longer be assumed to be linked to physical possession, and that collaborative approaches involving multiple parties and diverse roles will need to be explored.

The concept of an original has traditionally been associated with a value that comes from uniqueness, age or rarity. Traditional collections are driven by possession of originals. This is being stretched beyond recognition in the digital world. Replication of digital resources is relatively easy in the short term. Back-ups and downloading protocols deliver versions which are, in effect, indistinguishable from the original. Digital resources exist in many places – in back-ups, replicated on many servers across networks, perhaps in multiple versions. Indeed, redundant storage in multiple locations is a digital preservation strategy being pursued within the LOCKSS Project (Lots of Copies Keep Stuff Safe, www.lockss.org). Within the entertainment industry, the attempts to control peer-to-peer file sharing of music, film and photos is perhaps an illustration of the challenges that such replication, enabled by the technology, poses for traditional business models. At their base, all digital resources can be reduced to sequences of 1s and 0s, and, as identified earlier, there is a question about whether some resources actually exist independently of the act of viewing.

So what then, in preservation terms, is an original digital resource? What needs to be preserved for the long term? Is it the spirit of the original performance of that resource, that is, the look and feel of the original? Is it the original bits and bytes that comprise the resource? This stretching of the concept of 'original' is particularly challenging for museum professionals striving to maintain digital art. Just what is it that is being preserved – the original program, the experience of the viewer, the performance of the components? Is 'graceful obsolescence' part of the concept of the piece? The analogy is currently being made to performance art preserved at least in part through artists' instructions on what will constitute an appropriate rendition of the performance. The intention of the artist is deemed paramount, with museums seeking the active involvement of the digital artist in determining what preservation techniques will suit the work (Depocas et al., 2003; Rinehart, 2000).

In pulling apart traditional notions such as ownership and original, we are beginning to find a network of more granular concepts that need to be negotiated. Roles and responsibilities, relationships and context are becoming critical to how we document and preserve the digital resources we are charged with. And even here, different ways of viewing the world are emerging. The overwhelming urge is to keep things simple. But in the digital world, keeping things simple may not protect the very things that make the digital resources worth keeping.

This delicate balancing act between the simple and the complex is nowhere more manifest than in the data models behind the management of digital resources. The simple in this case is represented by the flat information resource discovery or cataloguing model of the Dublin Core community, where no actual data model is articulated and consequently some very strange things can arise. Because of its simplicity, the Dublin Core metadata is widely deployed. But within the preservation, cultural heritage and record-keeping communities the data models being used to support management of digital resources are increasingly relational – not one dimensional, but looking to view an object bound by various relationships into context with other objects, with people and with events. The movement away from the simple into the more complex models brings with it a tension – simple is easily implementable, but simple might not be right or appropriate.

## Specific digital preservation approaches

In a rapidly changing field it would only be the very brave who would assert that any of the digital preservation strategies currently being investigated are 'the answer'. Indeed, general consensus seems to be that adopting a spectrum of the strategies is the best practice that can be adopted at the moment (OCLC–RLG PREMIS Working Group, 2004).

Despite this word of caution, there are a number of approaches which have been tested in research and are now being incorporated into implemented practice. The two most prominent strategies are emulation and migration.

*Emulation* involves preserving the original digital object in the software and technical environment in which it was created, and, when required, a program is written or invoked in the current operating environment which emulates, or imitates, the operation, functionality and look of the original object. This is a technique derived from the online games community, where the experience of playing games written for now obsolete hardware and software, such as arcade computers, is recreated on today's computers. Emulation has been tested and proven in projects such as CAMilEON (www.si.umich.edu/CAMILEON/), but sceptics raise issues such as the expense of writing the many potential interfaces to the original software, and the performance of the original has raised concerns. Even within the games community, some authors of the original games assert that the performance offered by the emulators does not give an authentic enough feel of the original (Lynch, 2004). This is an issue for digital artists also (see Solomon R. Guggenheim Museum, 2004).

*Migration* is the strategy that, while preserving the original, copies and upgrades the digital resource into formats which can be read in the new versions of software or into software that will operate in new environments. This strategy, too, is not without its critics. All of us will have had the experience of opening an old word-processing document containing tables, footnotes or images in a newer version only to find that the formatting, links and look of the original are changed. This type of uncertainty about what functionality and data will be lost over the generational changes of software is multiplied many times over significant volumes of material when migration is pursued as a preservation strategy. Is the migrated version authentic? How do we document the loss? What degree of loss is appropriate? And so on.

The third strand to the preservation strategies is adopting a standardized format in which resources will be accepted or maintained. A large number of variations exist under this umbrella, from 'normalization' into a preservation format (e.g., National Archives of Australia's Xena Initiative (2004)) to determining a limited number of formats for acceptance into a digital repository, or mandating a specific format for capture (typically Adobe PDF). A further variation attempts to define a trustworthy digital object able to run on a universal virtual computer, which can be specified within a known environment (Gladney, 2005).

All of these strategies are just that, strategies. None of them offers a complete solution. Emulation involves the continual development and deployment of intermediary software to interpret original resources in a potential plethora of formats. Migration involves continual attention and monitoring of formats and versions of software to identify trigger points for performing the migration process and this will not be a one-off, but a continuing process. Adopting standardized formats will involve an initial transformation of the resource, then the deployment of either or both migration or emulation over time.

All of the strategies are heavily dependent upon the use of structured metadata, making our communities' response and willingness to embrace metadata strategies quite critical.

## Challenging professional practice

Digital resources and their long-term management inevitably create challenges to the way cultural heritage professionals undertake their professional roles. The methods and procedures to deal with physical objects are well established. The practice of preservation is almost able to be considered separately from other processes, such as acquisition, description (cataloguing) or use mediation. But this changes in the digital world. As one commentator has put it, 'we don't have a good consensus on what we're trying to accomplish through preservation, and the farther away our digital object drifts from behaviour that is rooted in physical artefacts the more uncertain we get' (Lynch, 2004, 610).

The fragility of digital resources, the need for attention to software and hardware dependencies from the time of their creation, is moving the role of preservation away from being a separate process undertaken in a time sequence removed from many other professional practices, to a process which is increasingly integral to all collection management practices. Application of preservation techniques is required to ensure access in the medium term (and this may be as little as five years), so the requirement to address preservation is not limited to those institutions dedicated to long-term cultural heritage. Attention to links, identification, formats and location is required on an ongoing basis. Preservation considerations and attention cannot now be left to the end.

The process of selection of what digital resources will be collected or acquired by cultural heritage institutions must be more clearly focused and conscious of preservation issues. This is not only to ensure that any agreements (explicit or implicit) for preservation can be met, but also to ensure that the formats selected can be managed. It may be that an institution determines that only selected format material will be accepted, because realistically, only a few formats can be managed within the institution. There are two schools of thought on the acquisition of digital resources. The first adopts a sweep first and sort later approach, where gathering or identifying all relevant resources is done and quality checking and layers of responsibility for long-term accessibility are completed at a later time, after the resources are in custody. Many of the web spidering techniques used to harvest web pages within libraries adopt such an approach. The second approach is more akin to a well formulated (and hence with greater up-front costs) collecting policy which articulates quite precisely what resources will be targeted as the institution's responsibility and, once accepted, the preservation responsibility is assumed. There is danger in the undifferentiated sweep of resources. The Internet Archive, for example, employs this technique, but does not seek permission from the owners of the resources for the gathering, while specifying a protocol for nominating specific pages off-limits to the crawlers. Recently, it has been subject to legal proceedings, alleging that the access to old web pages, stored in the Internet Archive's database, was unauthorized and illegal, and claiming copyright infringement, violation of the Digital Millennium Copyright Act, and violation of the Computer Fraud and Abuse Act (Roberts, 2005).

In the digital world, content is being unbundled from known containers (OCLC, 2004). Re-use of information content is paramount; the forms in which the content are displayed, moved and manipulated are not static. The technological environment which allows this flexibility treats content as king. But for all cultural heritage professionals, context is critical. What exists in one context may be completely innocuous and uninteresting, while in a different context that exact same content may be critically important. A much greater emphasis on documentation of context is required to enable meaningful interpretation of content in both the short and long term. In the paper world, particularly for library professionals, much of the cataloguing-in-publication work undertaken by co-ordinated national systems removed the need for individual resource cataloguing in specific institutions. As digital resources are created outside the boundaries of such established publications systems, the need to readdress context documentation becomes critical.

There is an additional role emerging with the importance of provenance and authenticity of digital resources in the electronic world. Where duplicates abound, clones can be readily made and content easily manipulated without apparent trace, the ability to verify or act as a trusted source for digital resources is a role suggested for cultural institutions into the future. Resources in their repositories may not be unique, but they are accompanied with appropriately documented contextual detail and verified as being authentic. Archives, of course, have always had this role, but now it seems that the importance of these fundamental concepts is becoming integral to all cultural heritage institutions.

The role of the information professional in performing a mediation service to users - assisting in the information provision tailored to specific needs - seems to be diminishing in public demand with the advent of the powerful searching engines operating on the web, such as Google, Yahoo, etc. Users are no longer location-dependent, and demand ubiquitous 24/7 access to all information resources. The role and rethinking of the role of reference mediator is also in transition.

Another emerging role is that of the enabler of long-term access. Again, custody or physical possession of the digital resource is not absolutely essential for a cultural heritage institution to perform this role. The world of networked computing over-rides the requirement to house the resource in one single place. However, negotiating the responsibilities to ensure that access to digital resources in the long term is possible regardless of where they live, may well be a role undertaken by cultural heritage institutions. It is a new version of a much older role and one that cannot be practically undertaken by cultural heritage institutions on their own, but must be done in collaboration.

Rights in information resources are becoming increasingly financially valuable where repackaging the old in new ways may provide income streams to businesses that previously were quite happy to relinquish older material to a collecting institution. Indeed, the technologies for protecting access and ensuring security are well deployed for managing digital resources while they are in formation. Paradoxically, some of the techniques employed to protect access and security, such as encryption and password protection, can work as inhibitors to effective preservation. Storing encrypted records within organizational or institutional storage may be a technologically feasible solution for controlling access effectively in the short term, but to provide longer-term access beyond the holder of the specific cryptographic key, it requires management of a complex framework of public and private keys. A small-scale example of the potential problems is the case of the Norwegian Reidar Djupedal, who managed the Ivan Assen Centre of Language and Culture and had indexed over 11,000 titles by the time of his unexpected death. He had password protected the database on which this information was stored. The case made international news after the Director appealed for the assistance of the worldwide hacking community to break the password and enable access. The hackers achieved this in under five hours, whereas re-doing the work would have taken over five years (Beagrie, 2005).

The importance of appropriately structured and quality metadata is critical to many of the preservation strategies and management processes already discussed. As the importance of metadata creation and management as a component of digital resource management becomes more accepted across our community, much greater clarity is being achieved in the specification of metadata for specific resource types and purposes. As indicated, the human preference for the simple is being replaced by an understanding that managing complexity is essential in the digital world if we are to fulfil our cultural mandate. But to achieve implementation of complex metadata requirements, we need to change some of our understandings of metadata. It is not possible to manually create the complex metadata being specified for cultural heritage resources. Much of it will be inherited from elsewhere, or linked to other sources of metadata. It will be used to drive automatic processes and at the same time those processes will create more metadata. The old 'cataloguing' mindset relating to metadata must change in this digital world, if strategies built upon metadata deployment are to succeed.

## Implemented initiatives and experience

In one area considerable institutional progress can be reported. The adoption of the Open Archival Information System (OAIS) reference model, both as an International Standard (ISO 14721:2003) and as one of the critical infrastructure tools for building digital repositories is a unifying protocol. The OAIS reference model defines the basic functional components of a system dedicated to the long-term preservation of digital information, details the key internal and external system interfaces, and characterizes the information objects managed by the system (Lavoie, 2004). There have been questions as to whether it meets archives and record-keeping requirements (Hofman, 2002), but it has been widely adopted as a benchmark in repository standards.

A number of libraries have been forced by the changing publishing environment around academic resources to provide infrastructure which allows self-archiving of publications by academics. Institutional repositories are now gaining a significant presence, particularly in the academic environment. Typically, these initiatives are currently using either Fedora (Flexible Extensible Digital Object and Repository Architecture, developed initially by Cornell University) or DSpace (developed by Massachusetts Institute of Technology and Hewlett Packard). Both initiatives are open source, facilitating up-take in peer institutions. With the use of the Open Archive Initiative's metadata harvesting protocol to enable sharing of resources across institutions, the academic community is coming closer to establishing a scholarly network not reliant on external publishers. While not immediately focused on digital preservation *per se*, these initiatives are important in that they are creating pools of significant expertise in the management of digital resources in a standardized fashion.

The presence of a variety of very feasible, institutionally based digital library implementations also begins to counter suggestions that digital libraries and preservation are so expensive and difficult that only one such institution per country can be economically supported for the long term. While this is a debatable proposition, different thinking about whether every institutional repository can maintain the dedicated resources required to satisfactorily address digital preservation is still open for debate. Various commentators have suggested that collaborative arrangements must be developed for providing preservation services, both physical and digital, in a world of diminishing resources.

A recent survey of digital preservation initiatives showed that actual experience in cultural heritage institutions was limited but trends indicate a widespread practice of storing metadata redundantly in XML or a relational database, use of the METS (Metadata Encoding and Transmission Standard) metadata for non-descriptive metadata, use of the OAIS model as the base for functional specification of software, a combination of software applications and maintaining multiple versions of resources with complete metadata for all versions (OCLC/RLG PREMIS Working Group, 2004).

## Conclusion

As we become more aware of the issues of preserving digital resources which are fundamentally fragile in the long term, it is not sufficient to stand back and take a passive view or wait to get involved until 'the answer' is clear. Society expects our cultural institutions to preserve appropriate traces of our conduct across a broad spectrum of endeavour. As a general statement, society as a whole has yet to appreciate the strains that digital preservation puts upon our institutions in fulfilling our mandates. The technology which works so brilliantly for access in the short term builds a superficial patina of expectation that it will be equally easy for long-term access.

Preservation of digitally born resources poses significant challenges for cultural heritage institutions, which are poorly articulated even within our own professional groups. However, there is considerable hope that digital preservation will become a recognized and fundworthy mission. Some of this change will come with experience in digital preservation implementations and the viability of models currently featured in research. But the largest area of hope is the fact that with digital photography becoming ubiquitous, every happy snapper is now a stakeholder in solving the problems of digital preservation. Our institutions should take heart from this broadening of the stakeholder base and be at the forefront of advocating the broader agenda of maintenance of digital cultural heritage resources for the long term.

# References

ABC Radio (2001) *Knowledge Indignation: road rage on the information superhighway*, (12 August),
www.abc.net.au/rn/talks/bbing/stories/s345514.htm.

Adams, M. O. and Brown, T. E. (2000) Myths and Realities about the 1960 Census, *Prologue*, **32** (4),
www.archives.gov/publications/prologue/2000/winter/1960-census.html
[accessed October 2005].

Beagrie, N. (2005) Plenty of Room at the Bottom? Personal digital libraries and collections, *D Lib Magazine* (June),
www.dlib.org//dlib/june05/beagrie/06beagrie.html
[accessed October 2005].

CAMiLEON Project (2002), *BBC Domesday*,
www.si.umich.edu/CAMILEON/domesday/domesday.html
[accessed October 2005].

Depocas A., Ippolito, J. and Jones, C. (eds) (2003) *Permanence through Change: the variable media approach*, New York, NY, Guggenheim Museum,
http://variablemedia.net/e/preserving/html/var_pub_index.html
[accessed October 2005].

Gladney, H. (2005) *Trustworthy 100 year Digital Objects: durable encoding for when it's too late to ask*, Glasgow, ERPANET (Electronic Resource and Preservation Network),
http://eprints.erpanet.org/7/ [accessed October 2005].

Hofman, H. (2002) Review: some comments on preservation metadata and the OAIS model, *Digicult.Info* 2, (October), 15–20,
www.digicult.info/downloads/digicult_info2.pdf
[accessed October 2005].

Lavoie, B. F. (2004) *The Open Archival Information System Reference Model: introductory guide*, Heslington, Digital Preservation Coalition,
www.dpconline.org/docs/lavoie_OAIS.pdf [accessed October 2005].

Lynch, C. (2004) Preserving Digital Documents: choices, approaches and standards, *Law Library Journal*, **96** (4), 609–17,
www.aallnet.org/products/2004-40.pdf [accessed October 2005].

National Archives of Australia (2004) *Digital Preservation Software Applications*,
www.naa.gov.au/recordkeeping/preservation/digital/applications.html

[accessed October 2005].

OCLC (2004) *2004 Information Format Trends: content, not containers,*
www.oclc.org/reports/2004format.htm. [accessed October 2005].

OCLC-RLG PREMIS Working Group (2004) *Implementing Preservation Repositories for Digital Materials: current practice and emerging trends in the cultural heritage community,*
www.oclc.org/research/projects/pmwg/surveyreport.pdf
[accessed October 2005].

Rinehart, R. (2000) The Straw that Broke the Museum's Back? Collecting and preserving digital media art works for the next century, *Switch*, issue 14 (14 June), http://switch.sjsu.edu/nextswitch/switch_engine/front/front.php?artc=233 [accessed October 2005].

Roberts, J. (2005) Discovery or Hacking? Law firms test boundaries, *Law Office Computing,* (November),
www.lawofficecomputing.com/EDC/eloc/november05/news01.php
[accessed November 2005].

Solomon R. Guggenheim Museum (2004) *Echoes of Art: emulation as a preservation strategy,*
www.variablemedia.net/e/echoes/ [accessed October 2005].

Stuckey, S. (1991) The Good Oil for Australia. In Reed, B. and Roberts, D. (eds), *Keeping Data: papers from a workshop on appraising computer-based records*, Sydney, Australian Council of Archives and Australian Society of Archivists.

# CHAPTER 9

# Preserving cultural heritage in times of conflict

René Teijgeler

## Introduction

There are many professionals who on a daily basis struggle to safeguard all that the human mind produces, tangible as well as intangible products. Most of the time conservators try to protect our heritage against the natural process of deterioration. They fight the acidity of paper, the copper corrosion of miniatures, the chemical burning of leather, the shrinkage of overheated parchment, the disintegration of red silk or the yellowed varnish of paintings. At most, they can only stop these destructive processes temporarily as, in the end, nature will overcome all of our tangible heritage: all is lost that is delayed.

Next to the inevitable natural causes of decay, natural hazards such as earthquakes, floods, landslides, wildfires, tsunamis and tropical cyclones exact a heavy toll in terms of direct loss and irreparable damage to our cultural legacy. The consequences of the tsunami in Asia in 2004, the Katrina hurricane during the 2005 Atlantic season and the earthquake in northern Pakistan just before the severe winter of 2005/2006, were first of all horrifying because of the huge loss of human lives, but at the same time left entire regions devoid of libraries, archives and museums.

Manmade disasters can even outdo natural disasters in the detrimental effects on our collective memory of the past. Theft, war, civil disorder, terrorism, neglect and vandalism are human factors in the accidental or wilful destruction of our heritage (Teijgeler, 2001). Of these threats, armed conflict remains particularly intractable and disturbing. Regrettably, of late we have experienced more than once how shocking the effects of a violent struggle can be on the heritage of countries such as the former Yugoslavia, Afghanistan and Iraq. Statues are blown up because they are considered an insult to the 'only and right religion', archaeological sites are occupied by foreign troops and destroyed in the process, and archives are deliberately obliterated as part of an ethnic cleansing policy. Undoubtedly, the final decade of the 20th century was marked by destruction of heritage on a symbolic scale that has been unrivalled for the past several centuries.

Should the heritage worker take the ruinous effects of war, the ultimate failure of the human mind (Müller, 2005), as a fact of life or is there a way we can prevent the demolition of our cherished treasures? No, beyond personal responsibility it is not the primary task of cultural heritage management to prevent or stop war. Admittedly, heritage institutions play an increasingly important role in post-conflict situations, but they are unable to bring a halt to an armed conflict. Politicians declare war and soldiers wage war. Nevertheless, what cultural institutions can do is to prepare themselves for the event of war.

The increasing number of natural disasters in Europe during the 1990s exposed both the vulnerability of significant cultural assets and the lack of preparedness of local emergency services. Most countries were simply not prepared to protect their own history. As a result of the calamities, needs assessments were carried out, manuals written and regional co-ordination programmes initiated in order to be ready for future disasters; many countries apparently had to learn the hard way. In these risk management plans, most of the attention was focused on natural disasters; hardly any attention was paid to man-made disasters, except for theft and burglary. Only a few cultural institutions (e.g., in the UK and Spain) incorporated a possible terrorist attack in their plans. The shock of 9/11 forced some planners to consider the realities of a new international and radically different security environment. It is worth mentioning that two days after the Twin Towers came down in 2001 the Federal Emergency Management Agency changed the statement in the fact sheet on terrorism (published on their website) that a terrorist attack in the USA remains possible, though unlikely (Teijgeler, 2001). Yet, on the whole it remains to be seen how many organizations adapted their plans. While heritage management staff are slowly getting used to the idea of a possible terrorist attack, the idea of war in their backyard is considered absurd in spite of the recent intrastate conflicts. This changing reality compels any responsible person working in the heritage field to at least have another look at their risk management programme. The all-important question is whether we can prepare for war at all. Many of the heritage workers in war-ridden countries were badly prepared. Still, we can surely learn a great deal from them. In general, one can conclude that in cases where the staff take appropriate measures in good time much damage to the collections can be prevented.

## Be prepared

Man-made disasters strike worldwide. On the whole, armed conflicts declined considerably over the last 15 years, yet international terrorism is still rising, and the poorest countries are suffering the most (Human Security Centre, 2005; Marshall and Gurr, 2005). It is estimated that at the beginning of the 21st century nearly a quarter of the world's population was facing some type of crisis or post-conflict situation, and that two-thirds of the poorest countries were suffering as a result of current or recent conflicts (Malloch Brown, 2003). In the course of time, every country is confronted with damage to their cultural heritage as a result of either wilful or accidental destruction. It is unfortunate that local authorities and communities, especially those in tight economic circumstances, do not understand the benefits to be gained by reducing losses today for an unknown tomorrow (Gavidia, 2001). Clearly, one of the lessons learned in heritage preservation from the Iraqi Freedom Campaign in 2003 is, according to Ann Hitchcock (2003, 36), that 'an emergency operations plan is critical to ensuring that emergencies do not turn into disasters. Not only do staff and visitors need to know what to do and where to go, but also staff need to know how to protect the collections'. This is crucial for the survival of any cultural institution; after all, what are we without our artefacts or documents? In short, disasters need to be managed in order to control them, or at least to mitigate the effects.

A Disaster Management Cycle should address issues relevant to all phases of the disaster cycle: preparedness, response, recovery, rebuilding, prevention and mitigation. Yet, it should be realized that each collection, each building and each situation is unique and that every institution has to prepare for disasters with its own unique plan. There is a vast literature on disaster preparedness: for an overview see Teijgeler (2001); for examples see Conservation OnLine (2005).

Analogous to the well-known Integrated Pest Management method for killing insects, the newest approach to calamities is Integrated Emergency Management, which refers to a complex series of interdependent skills, knowledge and experience. The plan has to be flexible, it has to work on a holiday weekend or in freezing weather conditions, and at any location. It will need to be tested against specific scenarios. It should also be integrated into an organization's everyday working structure, and the activities of different departments within an organization should be integrated. Lastly, there is a vital need to co-ordinate arrangements with other authorities and organizations. Major disasters will almost always span boundaries, and indeed may spread.

Though the circumstances under which the damages are inflicted are rather specific, there is no particular type of damage uniquely associated with armed conflict. Damage resulting from armed conflict, depending on the nature of the armaments employed and the possibilities of secondary damages linked to the conflict (e.g., fire, flood), may resemble the impact of any or all natural disasters. Significant damage caused by armed conflict includes: full or partial destruction by bombs, shells and associated fire of structures and contents; loss of stability, weather tightness, or both, as a result of shelling which only partly destroys walls and roofs; damage to objects, collections and significant interior fixtures and fittings by heat, smoke and combustion by-products; and water damage resulting from efforts to arrest fire (Stovel, 1998).

The disaster cycle could in the event of war be subdivided into actions to be taken before the outbreak of an armed conflict (pre-conflict), during the conflict (peri-conflict) and after the conflict (post-conflict). In terms of international development, most attention is paid to post-conflict situations and not so much to the two preceding phases. In the build-up to a conflict of arms, politicians should make sure that the international treaties protecting cultural heritage, should the fighting start, are signed. They should also press for the signing of the conventions that will facilitate the return of looted and stolen artefacts. Establishing contacts with international organizations will also be very advantageous in case of an emergency relocation of collections outside the country. International contacts will help the management to overcome their problems in all phases of the conflict but especially during the rehabilitation of the institution after the fighting stops.

The pre-conflict phase is also the time to start developing a contingency plan. These plans enable administrators to make choices in advance. It appears that in practice this is the most difficult part of the whole preparation strategy: deciding which part of the collection should be saved first or will require special attention. How do you determine the value of a book? Is the criterion the book's replacement value, or its popularity with readers, the uniqueness of the specimen, the artistic value or the cultural value? Under pressure, bad choices are often made and books are grabbed randomly from the shelves in order to save 'as many as possible'. That is exactly why we should make plans – to prevent chaos. It would be wise to learn from the hands-on experiences of our colleagues who had to see their cultural institution through an armed conflict. Reading about experiences of other institutions can not only help to avoid making the same mistakes but can give an idea of what to expect after a disaster.

## International law

There is much debate about the advantages and disadvantages of international law as a tool to prevent armed conflict and, consequently, to avert the danger of destruction of a nation's heritage. Some believe war is inevitable and part of human nature, and as such can be subject to humanitarian law. Others refuse to accept this notion for reasons of principle, and maintain that people should strive for a peaceful world where conflicts are resolved in a non-violent way – waging peace, not war.

Sadly, prohibiting wars has not prevented them from occurring. That is how humanitarian law came into being: to mitigate the most destructive effects of war. Humanitarian law is part of international law and seeks to protect victims of war and regulate hostilities. Its first aim is to protect the lives of individuals. But war is not only the enemy of man, it is also the enemy of the best that man has produced: the whole cultural and historic heritage (Toman, 1996). The tendency of recent warfare to move from interstate to intrastate has amplified the impact. The direct, indirect and cumulative impacts on cultural heritage have been devastating (Gergana, 2001). It appears that the scores for armed conflict, as a cause of destruction and damage for archives, are extremely high in most of the continents (van der Hoeven and Albada, 1996).

From time immemorial, war has gone hand in hand with widespread destruction and the 'right to booty'. The aim of war was to collect booty and thus the destruction of cultural property was considered an inevitable consequence of war. The first stirrings of a wish to protect works of art appeared during the Renaissance. The concept was further developed in the 16th and 17th centuries by writers on international law, such as Jacob Przyluski. In his '*Leges seu statuta ac privilegia Regni Polonaie* (Cracow, 1553) Jacob Przyluski [Jacobus Prilusius] ... put forward the idea that every belligerent should show regard for a work of art, but not solely because of its religious nature' (Toman, 1996, 4–5). The protection of cultural property was also considered in non-western civilizations. Under Islamic law, the obligation to distinguish between civilian and military objects is clearly imperative and permits no exception. In accordance with the orders of the first Caliph Abu Bakr (AD 632–634) attacks should be strictly confined to military targets (i.e. objects that by their nature or use are intended for the pursuit of hostilities). Thus the Islamic concept presumes all objects to be civilian unless proven otherwise (Toman, 1996).

## The Hague Convention

The Hague Convention of 1899 (for the complete text of the Convention with Respect to the Laws and Customs of War on Land, see www.icrc.org/ihl.nsf/INTRO/150?OpenDocument) and the Roerich Pact (http://sangha.net/roerich/roerich-pact.html) signed in Washington DC in 1935 were the first major international agreements to create measures designed to protect cultural property during war. They were followed by the Convention for the Protection of Cultural Property in the Event of Armed Conflict (http://portal.UNESCO.org/culture/en/ev.php-URL_ID=8450&URL_DO=DO_TOPIC&URL_SECTION=201.html), popularly termed the Hague Convention, adopted in 1954 at a conference in the Hague held under the auspices of UNESCO. This Convention was a response to the wide-scale destruction of cultural heritage during World War 2 and sought to ensure that cultural property, both movable and immovable, was safeguarded and respected as the common heritage of humankind. Cultural property and cultural institutions, as long as they were not put to military purposes, were to be protected in armed conflicts. The Convention's definition of cultural property is broad, including significant architectural monuments, art works, books or manuscripts of artistic or historical significance, museums, large libraries, archives, archaeological sites and historic buildings. The Convention was strengthened by the 1977 Additional Protocols of the Geneva Convention, relating to the protection of victims of international armed conflicts (http://www.icrc.org/web/eng/siteeng0.nsf/htmlall/genevaconventions?opendocument). Today 114 member states out of the 191 United Nations are signatories to the Convention. There are some prominent exceptions: the USA, the UK and Japan have yet to join, but recently the People's Republic of China (2000) and Canada (1998) joined the signatories.

According to reports submitted to the Director-General of UNESCO, breaches of the treaty have occurred in far too many cases in countries such as Turkey, Israel, Iraq and the states that were formerly part of Yugoslavia. The Hague Convention has been violated in such instances as the Turkish bombardment of Paphos, Cyprus, in 1974, and military operations in and around the archaeological site of Tyre during the 1982–83 conflict between Israel and the Palestine Liberation Organization in Lebanon. During the Iran–Iraq war of the 1980s, Iran reported Iraqi shelling of cultural and historic sites in Abadan and Shush. Iraq refused to mark its own sites with flags containing the emblem designated by the Convention 'because this emblem may be seen by aeroplanes not only by the missiles and artillery, which attack the Iraqi towns with no exception'. During the more recent conflict in the Persian Gulf, Iraq violated the Convention both in its placement of war planes at the archaeological site of Ur and in the looting by Iraqi forces of the 30,000-piece Islamic art collection in Kuwait's National Museum (Levin, 1992). The most blatant violations of the Hague Convention occurred during the clashes in Yugoslavia when even the Convention symbol, the Blue Shield placed on historic buildings for protection, was actually being used as a target for violence in 'cultural warfare and terrorism'.

During Operation Iraqi Freedom (2003) the USA claimed that they were acting along the lines of the Hague Convention (personal communication with the staff of the State Department, Bureau of Educational and Cultural Affairs, International Cultural Property Protection office in September 2004). Indeed, during the initial air raids the US air force managed to avoid damage to important heritage sites. The list of 5,000 ancient sites and monuments that was handed over to the Pentagon by the Oriental Institute of the University of Chicago two months before the invasion of Iraq seemed to have been taken into account (Gibson, 2003). Yet, as the occupation continued there were too many occasions that were certainly not in line with the Hague Convention. The most remarkable disasters were the failure of the US forces to protect the looting of museums, libraries and archives after the initial fighting was over (al-Radi, 2003b; Gibson, 2003), the continuous looting of the archaeological sites (Garen and Carlton, 2005) and the illegal occupation of the archaeological site of Babylon by the coalition forces (Curtis 2004; International Audit Commission, 2004).

In contrast to the numerous breaches of the Convention, many instances can be quoted when the Hague Convention did make a difference. As the Senior Consultant for the Ministry of Culture (Summer 2004 – Spring 2005), I was able to convince the coalition forces on several occasions to withdraw from important archaeological sites or monuments by referring to the Hague Convention. (For details on my role in the clearance of the military camp at the Babylon site, see Schwartz, 2005.) I also prevented extensive damage to the al-Hatra site by negotiating the reduction of the necessary nearby detonation programme by half, referring to the obligation of occupying forces to protect archaeological sites as stated in the Hague Convention. I called upon the same convention when arguing with the Deputy Chief of Mission about the historical and cultural value of the inner city of Najaf when the coalition forces were besieging the city. In one instance a local commander used the most infamous clause in the Hague Convention - the right to take over a cultural monument on the basis of 'military necessity' - but after two months of my working up and down the military chain of command the US army withdrew from the monument. This was the famous Malwiya minaret in Samarra, dating back to AD 852. Indeed, the tower was the highest point in the city and thus of strategic importance and a real vantage point for the soldiers to fight the insurgents who were attacking US soldiers. In January the insurgents shot at the soldiers on top of the tower, causing serious damage. When I finally managed to convince the commander to clear the minaret, he claimed he did not know the tower was that old. Admittedly, the outside of the minaret was restored in the 1990s, but 90% of the construction was close to 1,200 years old.

The conflicts of the 1980s and 1990s - when destruction of heritage became an element in campaigns of humiliation aimed at subjugating opposing ethnic groups - forced the international community to re-examine the Hague Convention, which had only partially addressed intrastate warfare. The result was the 1999 Second Protocol to the Hague Convention (www.unesco.org/culture/laws/hague/html_eng/protocol2.shtml), which strengthens the Convention and creates a new category of enhanced protection for cultural property deemed to be of the greatest significance to humanity. The Second Protocol also outlines measures for safeguarding cultural property to be undertaken in peacetime. These include:

> the preparation of inventories, the planning of emergency measures for protection against fire or structural collapse, the preparation for the removal of movable cultural property or the provision for adequate in situ protection of such property, and the designation of competent authorities responsible for the safeguarding of cultural property.

The protocol is a great improvement as it obligates the signatories to work on prevention of war damage to cultural heritage during peacetime. In fact, this is the opportunity for cultural institutions to extend their disaster preparedness plans with a section on how to avert war damage. With the

Second Protocol directors can easily convince the authorities to act upon this extended covenant, once their countries have become signatories. However, patience is required as the Second Protocol has so far only been signed by 35 states and only came into force in 2004.

## UNESCO and UNIDROIT

The massive looting and illicit trade of cultural collections in peri- and post-conflict situations can be stopped, at least partly, when both the 'producing' and the 'consuming' countries – respectively the countries of origin and the market countries – sign the 1970 UNESCO Convention on the Means of Prohibiting and Preventing the Illicit Import, Export and Transfer of Ownership of Cultural Property (http://portal.unesco.org/en/ev.php-URL_ID=13039&URL_DO=DO_TOPIC&URL_SECTION=201.html) and the 1995 UNIDROIT Convention on Stolen and Illegally Exported Cultural Objects (www.unidroit.org/english/conventions/1995culturalproperty/1995culturalproperty-e.htm). Though looting and illicit trade in art objects are often associated with archaeological objects, the uncovered treasures, the substantial looting of the libraries, archives and museums at the beginning of the Iraqi Freedom Campaign and the debate about the Schøyen Collection, a collection of extremely important Buddhist manuscripts illegally exported from Taliban Afghanistan, among others, show us that the holdings of cultural institutions are not spared.

Sometime after the Taliban came to power a collection of Buddhist manuscripts from Afghanistan was added to the Schøyen Collection, Norway, allegedly the largest private manuscript collection formed in the 20th century, comprising about 13,500 manuscripts and inscribed objects. The acquired Buddhist manuscripts are often referred to as the 'Dead Sea Scrolls of Buddhism'. The single largest group of manuscripts in the collection are thousands of fragments of possibly 1,400 Buddhist manuscripts reported in 2000 and 2001 to have been taken out of Afghanistan. The manuscripts were said to have been found in a cave close to Bamiyan, and may have come from a library that was damaged in the late 7th or 8th century. It is clear that this collection did not leave Afghanistan legally. Atle Omland's web page (http://folk.uio.no/atleom/manuscripts.htm) presents the current debate concerning the ownership of these and other manuscripts in the Schøyen Collection (see also Omland and Prescott, 2002; Prescott and Omland, 2003).

Besides the aforementioned Conventions, the Protocol of the 1954 Hague Convention (www.unesco.org/culture/laws/ hague/html_eng/page8.shtml) - in particular chapter X, article 1, subarticles 1-4 - also provides for the prevention of exportation of cultural property and the return of illegally exported property from an occupied territory. While the 1970 UNESCO Convention creates strategies between states to prevent illicit traffic and to promote co-operation on the return of cultural property, the 1995 UNIDROIT Convention ensures that private owners have direct access to the courts of another country where cultural property stolen from their owners is found. It also allows states to sue in the courts of such a country for important cultural property belonging to certain categories which has been illegally exported. For obvious reasons, the last treaty is heavily opposed by the antiques trade; the art dealers, in particular, worry about the fact that the onus of proof lies with the insured. That is perhaps the reason why so many market countries are reluctant to sign the 1995 UNIDROIT Convention - so far the treaty has only 26 signatories.

The 1970 UNESCO Convention, on the other hand, has already been signed by 109 of the 191 member states of the United Nations. The willingness to sign this treaty seems to have grown over the last years as 18 countries have signed up since 2000, including powerful countries such as the UK, Japan, Sweden, Denmark and Switzerland. Several other countries, such as Germany and the Netherlands, are making preparations to sign. The growing political lobby in Europe (Brodie et al., 2000) to sign both Conventions appears to have been quite effective for the 1970 UNESCO Convention, but not so much for the 1995 UNIDROIT Convention. For European countries, the implementation of Council Regulation (EEC) no. 3911/92 on the export of cultural goods and Council Directive no. 93/7/EEC on the return of cultural objects unlawfully removed from the territory of a member state are certainly of interest (http://europa.eu/comm/taxation_customs/customs/customs_controls/cultural_goods/index_en.htm).

When discussing the effectiveness of these treaties it is important to note that they provide the often poor countries of origin with legal instruments to claim the return of their stolen heritage. Of late, an increasing number of courts have sustained those claims, for example the June 2004 decision of the US Supreme Court in *Republic of Austria et al. v. Altmann*, which may open the doors of the US court system to a variety of long-standing claims against foreign governments (http://a257.g.akamaitech.net/7/257/2422/07june20041115/www.supremecourtus.gov/opinions/03pdf/03-13.pdf). Still, complicated conflict of law issues inevitably arise due to the wide variety of legal norms and the cross-border nature of most cultural property claims (International Bureau of the Court of Arbitration, 2004). Whether international law really changes the illegal trade in the market countries depends on the willingness of the nation states to implement these rules and regulations, but often charity begins at home.

## A case study: the international criminal tribunal for former Yugoslavia

For those of us whose professional life is focused on conserving heritage, it is painful to acknowledge that not only is our passion not shared by all, but that there are some in this world who can and will vigorously eradicate what we work to preserve (Whalen, 2001). Most in modern society, however, believe that these practices are no longer acceptable. Today, the deliberate destruction of cultural property, in the absence of over-riding military necessity, is a serious violation of international law and those responsible for ordering and carrying out such attacks can be prosecuted for war crimes. The Nuremberg Trials after World War 2 marked the first time that individuals were held accountable for cultural war crimes. Several Nazi officials were sentenced to death for a plethora of violations that included the destruction of cultural property.

Following that precedent, the International Criminal Tribunal for Former Yugoslavia (www.un.org/icty/) was empowered to prosecute individuals deemed responsible for the 'seizure of, destruction or wilful damage done to institutions dedicated to religion, charity and education, the arts and sciences, historic monuments and works of art and science'. Whether 'seizure' in this case covers the intentional removal of museum art objects from museums in Kosovo to Belgrade is uncertain. It could be argued that, at the time these items were taken, the Serbian Ministry of Culture had legitimate jurisdiction over the museums. Precedents are not encouraging in this regard. Almost nine years after Serbian museum professionals were sent from Belgrade to 'evacuate' the art collection of the Vukovar Museum to Serbia, and nearly five years after the end of hostilities, not one of those items has been returned to the Croatian museum which owns them (Riedlmayer, 2000b). The indictments of Slobodan Milosevic for the 1991 attacks by the armed forces of Yugoslavia on the ancient city of Dubrovnik, Croatia, included one for the destruction of historic monuments (www.un.org/icty/indictment/english/mil-ii011008e.htm). What made matters worse was the fact that two of the bombed monuments were protected under the terms of the Hague Convention and seemed to have been deliberately targeted (Brodie, 2003). The former Yugoslav president and other officials were also indicted for the destruction of cultural and religious heritage in Kosovo. We cannot but conclude that during and after the conflict the belligerents did not respect *volens nolens* the text or the nature of the Hague Convention.

While the 1954 Hague Convention requires that protected monuments be designated and marked as such, the 1977 Protocols I and II Additional to the Geneva Conventions of 1949 use a more inclusive wording, which is also reflected in the tribunal's statute. Furthermore, it was evident that the criteria employed in listing monuments for protection by the Serbian authorities before the war had been conditioned to a considerable extent by ideological considerations (Herscher and Riedlmayer, 2000). The Conventions related to cultural war crimes, however, do not spell out the penalties that should be handed down for violations (Maass, 1999).

In this global era there is still a 'future' for warring states, and no humanitarian law will be able to prevent that. But multilateral treaties and conventions will certainly make a difference and at least protect part of the world's heritage. In the preliminary results of a recent survey, approximately 80% of the respondents, when asked to judge its importance, held the view that 'accidents, damage and loss can be prevented by providing appropriate legal protection at the local, regional, national and international level', while fewer (58%) felt that it could be achieved without difficulty. (The Conservation Management Questionnaire is part of the PhD research of Jeremy Donald Hutchings at University College London, and the first results will be published in late 2006.) Apparently, many heritage workers believe in the ability of international law to protect cultural heritage in times of armed conflict.

## Risk preparedness

Some of the cultural institutions saw the violent conflict in their country coming and prepared themselves to the best of their abilities, considering the local circumstances. The institutions that managed to save their collection, or part of it, had prepared themselves *before* the conflict broke out. Sometimes it was done in a systematic way but it was also not uncommon for the measures to be taken haphazardly. At the same time the practical experiences of our colleagues show us how creative they can be when the situation is dire. That is why risk preparedness, as part of a bigger risk management plan, should start to look at the measures that can be taken *before* a conflict breaks out. In other words, cultural heritage institutions should develop a strategy for the protection of cultural heritage in the event of an armed conflict. The Second Protocol of the Hague Convention (1999) will give the management the legal back-up to do so. The guiding principle in the development of such plans should, without a doubt, be that 'local problems need local solutions'. All too often solutions from developed countries are chosen to address problems in developing countries.

## Closedown

A normal practice listed in every disaster preparedness plan is to close down the institution as soon as possible in case of emergency. This is to prevent casualties rather than to safeguard the collection, as the iron rule in risk management is to put the interests of human beings before those of the collections. Once the doors are shut, the staff can pay full attention to securing the holdings.

Three weeks before the American invasion in March 2003, the staff of the Iraq Museum closed the galleries to the public and began the task of protecting the museum and its contents (al-Radi, 2003b). They were able to save important parts of the collections but they could not prevent the looting of 15,000 art objects at the unprotected museum. During the Gulf War (1990-91) the Iraq Museum was closed down only after the Ministry of Communications - located across the road from the museum - was bombed, and the resulting tremors shattered a number of the museum's showcases. Believing the war was not going to last long, the staff wrapped the displayed artefacts and locked them in the basement. However, they were wrong and in the end the stored objects disintegrated owing to inundation of the floor (Ghaidan and Paolini, 2003).

Unfortunately, the National Library and Archives of Iraq did not take any precautions before the American troops entered Baghdad. The employees simply did not show up and the building was left to the looters and set on fire. This resulted in a 60% loss of the state archives' records and documents, and a 25% loss of the library's book collection (Johnson, 2005). The new director of the Academy of Science and Technology in Baghdad was an unwilling eyewitness during the Gulf War when a pillaging mob entered the campus of the University of Basra, of which he was the dean, and ransacked most of the buildings, including the libraries. Even so, he was unable to convince his predecessor at the Academy to close the premises and safeguard the repository when the plunder started in 2003. After the crowd moved on, the library was left with 75% of its collections (personal communication with the director of the Academy of Science and Technology, Baghdad, October 2004).

The Kabul Museum in Afghanistan was officially closed down by the Najibullah Government (1986-92) because of increasing fears of an armed conflict and all objects were prepared to be moved (Grissmann, 2003). A decade later the collection was totally destroyed during the Taliban regime. Nonetheless, the Najibullah Government made the right decision.

## Safe haven

Once the institution is closed there are several options to secure the holdings, depending how much time is left. One option is to move (part of) the collections to safer premises outside the institution or even outside the country. Of course, such an operation takes time. Again this stresses the importance of a solid contingency plan in which an evacuation is anticipated. Usually the library, archive or museum has sufficient space in a building that is not too far away. An institution in a conflict-prone area should seriously consider relocating the collection outside the region: a project that can be realized with the help of international organizations. However, often the mistake is made of transferring materials to surroundings that do not meet the minimum preservation standards.

## Lebanon

In the first years of the Civil War (1975-90) the collection of the National Library of Lebanon, founded in 1921, was relatively safe though in poor condition. In 1979 the Government ordered the evacuation of the entire collection to the UNESCO headquarters in Verdun, France. Later the 3,200 boxes were returned to Lebanon and stored in Sin al Fil, a suburb of Beirut. There they lay for 15 years until the 200,000 books and documents were unearthed and saved from dreadful climate conditions. What was left was sent to the better climatized depots of the University of Lebanon, southeast of Beirut (Lebanese National Library Rehabilitation Project, n.d.). It is not clear why the books were moved from France back to Lebanon.

The National Museum of Lebanon in Beirut was set up in the 1920s and housed the major part of the collection of the Antiquities Department, as well as finds from excavation sites. The building is situated on the corner of a very important junction of three major arteries that lead into the city. In the early days of the Civil War, the director ordered staff to send all the items that they had no room for in the warehouses to the Department's stores in other parts of Beirut and some of the valuables to the Central Bank (Erlich, 2003). The small precious objects, the gold and other major pieces, were shipped to the French Archaeological Institute in Damascus for safe-keeping. Other objects were placed in the underground chambers of the Crusader Castle in Byblos, north of Beirut. The remaining objects stayed in the museum and were later buried (al-Radi, 2003a).

## Iraq

Another example that clearly shows us that relocating the collection is not always enough is the move of the Ottoman Archives in Iraq. This old archive, one of the few that survived the war, was rescued from the flooded cellars of the Ministry of the Interior in 2003. The 42,000 documents from the Ottoman and Royal eras were packed in 156 metal boxes and placed in cold stores, part of the kitchen of the former Senior Officer's Club. Since the electricity was constantly interrupted the temperature fluctuated from 0° C to 8° C, which caused a mould explosion. The only way to stabilize the documents was to deepfreeze them. They were repacked in acid-free boxes, loaded on to a freezer truck and transported to the premises of the National Library where the truck was parked under a shelter to protect it from the sun and flying bullets. Two generators supplied the necessary electricity (Teygeler, 2005).

The story of the evacuation of the Iraqi Jewish Archive to the US National Archives and Records Administration (NARA) demonstrates that a transfer across borders can be highly political and sensitive. Rare, historic and modern books, documents and parchment scrolls pertaining to the Iraqi Jewish community were found in the flooded basement of the Iraqi Intelligence (Mukhabahrat) headquarters in Baghdad in early May 2003. Upon removal from the basement, the wet materials were packed into sacks and transported to a nearby location where they were partially dried, after which the materials were placed in 27 metal trunks. The Coalition Provisional Authority (CPA) arranged for the materials to be frozen, which served to stabilize their condition and prevent further mould growth. At the request of the CPA, conservators from the NARA assessed the condition of the materials and made recommendations for their preservation (Iraqi Jewish Archive, 2003; Lufkin, 2004). In order to protect the documents from further damage it was decided with the consent of the chairman of the State Board of Antiquities and Heritage (SBAH) to transfer the archive to depots in the USA. A Memorandum of Understanding (MOU) was signed on 19 August 2003 and was valid for two years. Later that year articles appeared in the Arab press saying that US forces had, with the help of the Israelis, kidnapped the archive and shipped it off to Israel. Once in a while those biased reports were published again but in the spring of 2005 opponents of the Iraqi Transitional Government used this information to pressurize the Government. After the MOU expired in the summer of 2005, and under pressure of public opinion, the Iraqis asked for the return of the archive. Negotiations started in the spring of 2005 and a new MOU will be signed in 2006 to continue the preservation activities in the USA in full co-operation with Iraqi conservators and to ensure the safe return of the archive to Iraq (personal communication with the director of the State Board of Antiquities and Heritage, Berlin, November 2005).

Efforts to save the extensive and highly valuable manuscript collection at the House of Manuscripts from the impending war began four months before the war and continued right up to the week immediately prior to hostilities in April 2003. In the course of these efforts, all 50,000 manuscripts were taken to an air-raid shelter, while the microfilms and the CD-ROMs were taken to different undisclosed locations. The protection measures were undertaken even though the staff did not have official Ministry permission (as a matter of fact the Minister of Culture asked them to slow down their efforts). Today, the shelter contains almost 800 steel trunks filled with precious handwritten books collected in the 1990s from libraries all over the country. On three occasions looters tried to force the doors open but to no avail. On each occasion people from the neighbourhood chased the looters away and burned their vehicles. The US forces who were granted access to the shelter demanded that the treasure be taken to the Iraq Museum. Again when the military vehicles showed up the local crowd prevented them from loading the trunks on to their trucks. Later the CPA confirmed that their current policy was not to duplicate protection services in situations where local security measures appear to be sufficient (al-Tikriti, 2003).

Once the heaviest fighting in Baghdad was over and plundering crowds took to the streets, Shiite clerics, helped by local residents, opened the doors of the National Library and loaded their pick-up trucks with anything they could lay their hands on. The books were soon piled up against the wall of the local mosque and guard posts were set up. Some of the archives were packed into boxes and scattered around Shiite neighbourhoods (al-Radi, 2003b). It is not precisely clear what has actually been saved from the National Library because a few days later the whole library went up in flames, including all the catalogues.

The vault of a bank is for obvious reasons a very popular site to temporarily preserve artefacts. Before the Gulf War the treasure of Nimrud, consisting of Neo-Assyrian gold jewellery excavated at Nimrud between 1988 and 1990, had been placed in the vaults of the Iraq Central Bank. It was never removed, and was found safe when a team of Iraqi officials and representatives from the US military opened the vaults in 2003. However, the vaults had unfortunately been flooded during the fighting in 2003, which particularly affected the ivory objects (al-Radi, 2003b; Ghaidan and Paolini, 2003). The vault of the Bank of Lebanon was also used, at least for some time, to stock rare manuscripts and documents from the National Library of Lebanon upon their return from France, while the bulk was stored at Sin al Fin (Lebanese National Library Rehabilitation Project, n.d.).

After the massive plundering of the museums, libraries and archives in the immediate aftermath of the US-led invasion in Iraq and the continual looting of archaeological sites, the State Board of Antiquities and Heritage (SBAH) tried to get back as much of the cultural property as possible. Most of the stolen art objects appeared on the black market in Europe and the USA. Nearly 1,400 artefacts, however, were confiscated at the border of Jordan and are kept in secret storehouses in Amman. As quite a few junior archaeologists were trained in Amman with the help of Jordan's Department of Antiquities, the SBAH decided to store the confiscated artefacts provisionally with their Jordanian colleagues and use them to train the aspiring Iraqi archaeologists and customs officers in Amman. Syria, Saudi Arabia and Kuwait also seized Iraqi art objects and will for now hold them in safekeeping on their territory in agreement with the SBAH (Jordan Times, 2004; Villelabeitia, 2005).

## Afghanistan

During the Soviet-backed Najibullah Government (1986–92) the Kabul Museum ordered all objects on exhibit, numbering around 600, to be brought down to the storerooms and prepared to be moved. To minimize the risk of concentrating the objects in one place, some trunks were moved to the Central Bank Treasury vault in the Presidential Palace, others to the Ministry of Information and Culture, while the rest remained in the various depots of the Kabul Museum itself (Grissmann, 2003).

At several points in the tragic history of modern Afghanistan, those in power constantly meddled with Afghanistan's heritage. In general, moving the holdings of a cultural institution when armed clashes are expected is a sensible thing to do. However, transferring collections because the new rulers need the building or for any other incomprehensible reason is very harmful because of frequent handling and continuous changes in temperature.

The contents of the Kabul Museum were constantly on the move. In 1979 the museum was abruptly ordered to move the contents from Darulaman into the large and deserted house of Mohammed Naim, next to the French Embassy in Kabul. The objects were piled up to the ceiling in every room, in hallways and in the basements. The library ended up in the garages. One year later everything was taken back to Darulaman. In 1989 the Najibullah Government (1986-92) transferred the collections of the Kabul Museum again as it was on the frontline and considered too vulnerable. The manuscripts and miniatures were transported to the National Archives, yet a few years later they ended up on the black market after all. Other art objects were stocked at the vault of the Central Bank Treasury or at the Ministry of Information and Culture, while some remained in the various depots of the Kabul Museum. Before the arrival of the Taliban in 1996 it was decided to house what was left of the rich collections after the destruction of the museum in 1992 and the looting in 1993 at the centrally located Kabul Hotel. Over 500 crates, trunks and boxes were again shifted in 1998, when the hotel became a Taliban guesthouse. They were stored on the ground floor of the Ministry of Information and Culture. In March 2001 the world watched in impotent shock as the Taliban not only dynamited the Bamiyan Buddhas, but also destroyed big pieces left in the Kabul Museum and vandalized the Ministry and the museum's storerooms. Trunks were forced open and objects smashed (Grissmann, 2003).

The 23 years of war that have ravaged Afghanistan's cultural heritage made some of the museums' staff think of their connections abroad. For many years the Kabul Museum had historical ties with the Guimet Museum in Paris. During the Taliban Regime (1996-2001) they asked their colleagues in Paris to take temporary charge of a number of collection pieces.

With the permission of the authorities, the Guimet Museum took care of art objects retrieved by the Society for the Preservation of Afghanistan's

Cultural Heritage (SPACH), while waiting for the situation to stabilize (Cambon, 2003). In 1999, an 'Afghan Museum in Exile' at the Swiss Afghanistan Institute in Bubendorf was set up with the help of UNESCO. At the request of both the Taliban in the south and the Northern Alliance, the museum was asked in 1998 to assist them in the protection of the artefacts of Afghanistan. This museum has been given the task of temporarily housing confiscated objects from the illicit art and antiquities trade until Afghanistan returns to more peaceful times. No articles may be purchased by the museum as this would be an encouragement to looters. It currently houses 3,000 pieces from Afghanistan (Bibliotheca Afghanica-Afghanistan Museum in Bubendorf, Switzerland, 2004; Recknagel, 2002).

## Safekeeping within the walls

Often there is not enough time to move the collection to a safe location outside the institution or the country, and this is certainly always the case in the absence of a contingency plan. Then, the only option is to find a solution within the building itself. In particular the art objects on display will need considerable attention as they lack the general safety of a depot and thus are considered the most fragile. Partly owing to a lack of time, the big objects will have to be protected *in situ*, while the small ones can be wrapped up, packed and transported to the storage rooms. Some of the museums displayed great ingenuity in preserving large objects from war damage. From the real-life cases we can learn that hiding small collections of objects of value can certainly be worthwhile. In this case the rule is that the fewer people who know about the secret stashes the better.

During the Gulf War of 1991 the staff of the Iraq Museum decided to move the artefacts from all 20 galleries to the basement of the museum's old store building after they were shattered as a result of the bombing of the Ministry of Communications, located opposite the museum. They wrapped the most fragile objects in cotton wool and the metal ones in rubber padding and placed them in metal trunks, believing the war would not last long. However, the bombs did not stop and the generators supplying the electricity were destroyed causing the floor to be flooded. The metal cases corroded, allowing humidity to reach the protective cotton wool and rubber padding and turn them into nesting grounds for bacteria, moulds and other harmful organisms. The employees were rendered helpless as the import of necessary chemicals was not authorized by the UN Sanctions Committee (Ghaidan and Paolini, 2003).

In March 2003 the staff of the Iraq Museum transferred most of the movable objects on show in the galleries to the underground storerooms. Metal gates in front of the doors were welded shut. The larger objects and statues were left in place, and foam rubber pads were placed in the area around them to protect them in case they fell off their pedestals. The rubber pads were also placed in front of the Assyrian Reliefs, and on the floors of all the storerooms. The staff hoped that these would protect the objects if a direct hit toppled the metal shelves. When US soldiers entered the museum after one month they noted that the protected art objects were much better off than those left unprotected (Bogdanos and Patrick, 2005).

Discussions were held as to whether the staff should protect and conceal the steel doors of the storerooms with additional cement or brick walls. The curator's argument was that if the museum received a direct hit from an incendiary bomb and the storerooms caught fire, the firemen would be unable to reach them in time to put the fire out. So the storerooms were given no further protection. It was a calculated choice, but it turned out to be the wrong one on this occasion (al-Radi, 2003a). The museum only suffered one direct hit, and it did not cause any damage to the collection. Yet, in the early days of April several groups of looters entered the museum and were able to carry off 15,000 objects. The door to the Museum Library was one of the few that were covered up with a brick wall and all the books deposited were saved (al-Radi, 2003b). Part of the collection was secured in different secret compartments inside the museum known only to the board of directors, and they were never found by the plunderers (personal communication with the director of the Iraq Museum, Baghdad, November 2004).

The wartime story of the National Museum has become part of Lebanese legend. The museum in Beirut was totally unprepared when the Civil War (1975-90) broke out. It was located right on the demarcation line. At the start of the conflict the objects that were not transported elsewhere were stored in cardboard boxes in the offices on the second floor while the more resilient objects were placed on shelves in the basement storage rooms (al-Radi, 2003a). As the fighting became more violent, the director, assisted by his wife and several employees, took the opportunity during a ceasefire to empty the display cases and hide them and thus was able to rescue most of the artefacts (Pharès, 2003). They took out all the exhibited antiquities, took photographs of them and put them in boxes after having made lists of them. Afterwards, they moved them (including the intricate gold statues) to underground storage areas, and covered them with earth for camouflage.

Only four people in Lebanon knew the location of the ancient artworks. One of those people who knew the true location of the museum collection bore a particular burden as rumours spread that he was personally profiting from the sale of the museum's works. All the items that they had no room for in the stores were transmitted to the Department's stores in other parts of Beirut and the valuables were taken to the Central Bank (Erlich, 2003). The large and immovable objects had to be left in place. A handful of people carrying bags of cement, plywood and rolls of thick sheets of plastic were seen going into the museum to work. The larger objects (the sarcophagi, the floor and wall mosaics and statues) – cumbersome to say the least – could not be moved, and so had to be protected *in situ*. The sarcophagi were encased in a box made of plywood planks – they were literally 'boxed' in. Then they built another plywood box and the space between the two 'boxes' was filled with cement. Once this cement had dried the whole 'box' was covered over with another, thicker layer of cement. The sarcophagi looked like large rectangular cement blocks. The large marble statues were protected in a similar manner. However, the floor mosaics needed another solution. They were covered with a sheet of thick plastic on which plywood planks were placed. Then cement was poured over the whole until nothing showed; the mosaic was completely hidden under cement. They could not, however, treat the vertical mosaics in a similar way. Luckily, they survived the war and only one was damaged. At one time the museum even served as a base for the Syrian Army, but nobody discovered the ancient sarcophagi or the mosaics. Yet, the objects left in the underground storage rooms fared very badly. The metal shelves had buckled and rotted from standing in fetid water for so many years. The objects were saturated with humidity and became very fragile. Rain had seeped into the building from the racecourse behind the museum, causing decomposition in that closed environment for 18 years. It took many years to complete the restoration of the objects in the museum (al-Radi, 2003a).

## Neglect

As with every social process, war is not a static event, but has a build-up phase and a winding-down phase. In the years preceding the armed conflict between different factions within one state, one culture dominates and oppresses the others over and over again. In these intrastate conflicts, cultural pluralism has become a problem, where increasing cultural differences lead to homogeneity. The culture and even the mere existence of a particular ethnic or religious group is increasingly threatened over the years. In the end, this may lead to ethnic cleansing and cultural war crimes, as in the former Yugoslavia. Entire collections are carried away to the cultural institutions of the dominant leaders. The budgets for culture in the subordinate regions are skimmed and the sector is cut to the bone. International boycotts also have unforeseen consequences for the culture sector. The UN sanctions for Iraq, for example, which were supposed to harm the country's economy, also had detrimental effects on all cultural institutions. It became extremely difficult for conservators to update their knowledge, acquire new equipment or proper materials. Most of the materials required were chemical products, the import of which into Iraq was forbidden (Ghaidan and Paolini, 2003). The Oil-for-Food Programme did not change that; on the contrary, it made things worse (United Nations Independent Inquiry Committee into the United Nations Oil-For-Food Programme, 2005). It should be clear that any programme for the protection of cultural property in times of conflict has to deal repeatedly with cultural institutions in decline, institutions that have suffered years of neglect. Ironically enough, at the same time this situation enables the institutions to start afresh. In many instances it provides the opportunity to replace outdated card-cataloguing systems with digital catalogues in conjunction with bringing the organization into the electronic age.

When Slobodan Milosevic, party leader of the federal state of Serbia and later President of the Republic of Serbia, announced an 'anti-bureaucratic revolution' in Kosovo in 1989, he in fact put the region under Serbian rule. The impact on Kosovo was drastic and not only were the political institutions abolished, but Albanian cultural autonomy was also drastically reduced. Priština University was purged, television and radio broadcasts in Albanian ceased and the only Albanian-language newspaper was banned. From 1996 until NATO intervened in 1999, Albanian separatists fought a guerrilla war with the Serbian and Yugoslav security forces. The Archive of Kosovo, built around 1970, was not damaged during the Kosovo Conflict (1989-99). The years of conflict were a decade of systematic neglect of all public services and institutions, including libraries and archives. Many of the present heads of archive services suggest that it was a deliberate policy of neglect (Riedlmayer, 2000a). Albanian staff of the Archive of Kosovo were, it is claimed, forced from their jobs on ethnic grounds from December 1990, and those who remained after this were not allowed to enter storage areas unless accompanied by a Serb. Other actions included the transfer of the Kosovar archival heritage – such as the housing of the City Archive of Priština in rather low-quality, damp basement accommodation at the Archive of Kosovo – and the removal of equipment in whole or part, including parts of microfilm equipment, and office transport. Financial records of the archive from 1990 to 1999 were also taken (Jackson and Stepniak, 2000).

As early as March 1991, records appear to have been deliberately removed. When the Serbs finally withdrew in 1999 public records and archives comprising almost the entire documentary base for the orderly functioning of government and society in Kosovo were removed; some municipal registries were even burned on the spot. The Ministry of Justice in Belgrade announced that public records in Kosovo had been removed to Serbia 'to prevent the Albanian secessionists from destroying or forging [them]' (Jackson and Stepniak, 2000). Meanwhile, hundreds of thousands of Kosovars, who were deprived of their personal documents when they were expelled in the spring of 1999, whose passports or licences have expired, who wish to register a marriage, buy or sell property, settle a legal dispute or claim an inheritance, are left stranded in a legal and documentary limbo (Frederiksen and Bakken, 2000; MacKenzie 1996; Riedlmayer, 2000a).

The situation of the archives in the Kosovo Conflict also applied to the libraries. At the beginning of October 1990, ethnic Albanian faculty and students were ejected by Serbian police from classrooms and offices, and the University of Priština became an apartheid institution reserved for ethnic Serbs only. At the same time, non-Serb readers were banned from the National and University Library and Albanian professionals were summarily dismissed from their positions at the libraries. The acquisition of Albanian-language library materials effectively ceased. No records and printed books relating to the Albanian community were acquired after 1990 and only 22,000 items were added to the collections in Kosovo in that period. A few years later a number of library facilities in Kosovo were converted to other uses. Parts of the National and University Library building in Priština were turned over to a Serbian Orthodox religious school; library offices were used to house Serb refugees from Croatia and Bosnia. For almost a decade, Kosovar Albanians, the majority of Kosovo's inhabitants, were not allowed to set foot inside their libraries. The Library's reserve collection – multiple deposit copies of publications in Albanian kept for exchange and for distribution to public libraries elsewhere in Kosovo – were gone; they had been sent to the Lipljan paper mill for pulping before the war by order of the Serbian library director (Riedlmayer, 1995, 2000a).

The Kosovar museums did not fare much better. The collections were despoiled, not by acts of deliberate destruction but by appropriation. Before the war in 1999, some of the more valuable items in the collections held by the religious communities in Kosovo – most notably the treasuries of the three major monastic institutions of the Serbian Orthodox Church – were reported to have been sent to the Museum of the Serbian Orthodox Church in Belgrade.

By order of the Serbian Ministry of Culture, hundreds of archaeological artefacts from three important museum collections in Kosovo – the Museum of Kosovo, the Municipal Museum in Mitrovice and the Regional Archaeological Museum in Prizren – were removed to Belgrade at the beginning of 1999, ostensibly for an exhibition. The small Gjakova museum had been closed to the public since 1990, and the Albanian staff were sent home. Unlike many other institutions in Kosovo, which had their archives shipped off to Serbia when Yugoslav troops withdrew at the end of the war, the Kosovo Museum has retained its working documentation, thanks to staff members who hid the files in their homes during the war (Riedlmayer, 2000b).

## Conclusion

The relatively recent examples given above illustrates some of the actions museums, libraries or archives can take at the threat of war. It goes without saying that even more tragic events can be quoted from earlier armed struggles, especially from the two World Wars in the 20th century. Some institutions were even destroyed twice. Consider the tragic fate of the ancient university of Leuven in Belgium. In World War 1 the library, dating back to 1438, was reduced to ashes. During the German invasion, within a few hours 300,000 books and 1,000 valuable manuscripts went up in flames. Rebuilding commenced immediately after the war and the first stone of the restored university library was laid in 1921. As fate would have it, the library was again burned to the ground in World War 2: this time 900,000 books were reduced to ashes. It took until 1951 before the ill-fated library partially re-opened and another ten years before the book stock reached its pre-war proportions. In World War 2 in particular, many collections, private and public, changed ownership illegally. Today the descendants of the victims are taking on whole nations and winning.

The dire fate of the libraries in the Baltic States is also catastrophic. Because of political upheavals, the Baltic States - Estonia, Latvia and Lithuania - saw their collections constantly changed and cleansed according to the desired history of the different occupiers. The Baltic States regained independence from the Russians in 1918, but the Russians invaded the region once more in 1940. They started to burn unwelcome titles until Nazi Germany took over in 1941. However, the Russians were able to continue their cleansing policy after 1945 when they defeated Nazi Germany. In 1991 the three Baltic nations re-declared their independence. They started to re-write their history and extended the library collections accordingly. Not only in Kosovo were precious books destroyed by sending them to the paper mill. The Nazis did the same with entire private libraries confiscated from Dutch Jewish citizens in World War 2 (Presser, 1965). Milan Kundera (1981, 159) puts it very well: 'the first step in liquidating a people is to erase its memory. Destroy its books, its culture, its history'.

Sadly, the wilful destruction of cultural property has a lengthy history. It should be clear from the above that it does make perfect sense to prepare for the future, even if it has many disasters in store for us. At least then our heritage has a chance to survive. The timely close-down of the cultural institution, the transfer of the collection to a safe haven (within the country or abroad), hiding the collection inside the institution: these are all actions that might well contribute to safeguarding our heritage, providing it is well packed and is stored under reasonable climatic conditions. Some of our colleagues were very inventive in finding solutions under pressure. Let us learn from them and prepare for the worst.

## References

al-Radi, S. (2003a) War and Cultural Heritage: lessons from Lebanon, Kuwait and Iraq, *De Kracht van Cultuur*, (October), http://kvc.minbuza.nl/nl/artikelen/war_and_cultural_heritage.html [accessed 14 October 2005].

al-Radi, S. (2003b) The Destruction of the Iraq National Museum, *Museum International*, **55** (3-4), 103-7.

al-Tikriti, N. (2003) *Iraq Manuscript Collections, Archives, & Libraries Situation Report, 8 June*, Oriental Institute, http://oi.uchicago.edu/OI/IRAQ/docs/nat.html [accessed 13 February 2006].

Bibliotheca Afghanica–Afghanistan Museum in Bubendorf, Switzerland (2004) *Afghanistan Cultural Profile*, www.culturalprofiles.org.uk/Afghanistan/Units/613.html [accessed 13 February 2006].

Bogdanos, M. and Patrick, W. (2005) *Thieves of Baghdad: one marine's passion for ancient civilization and the journey to recover the world's greatest stolen treasures*, New York, Bloomsbury.

Brodie, N. (2003) Stolen History: looting and illicit trade, *Museum International*, **55** (3-4), 10-22.

Brodie, N., Doole, J. and Watson, P. (2000) *Stealing History: the illicit trade in cultural objects*, Cambridge, UK, The McDonald Institute for Archaeological Research.

Cambon, P. (2003) The Role of the Guimet Museum in the Study and the Preservation of Afghan Heritage, *Museum International*, **55** (3-4), 54-61.

Conservation OnLine (CoOL) (2005) *Disaster Preparedness and Response*, http://palimpsest.stanford.edu/bytopic/disasters/ [accessed 7 November 2005].

Curtis, J. (2004) *Report on Meeting at Babylon 11th–13th December 2004*, London, British Museum www.thebritishmuseum.ac.uk/iraqcrisis/reports/Babylon%20Report04.pdf [accessed 14 December 2005].

Erlich, R. (2003) Lessons from Beirut on Bombed-out Art, *The Christian Science Monitor*, (21 August), 13.

Frederiksen, C. and Bakken, F. (2000) *Libraries in Kosova/Kosovo: a general assessment and a short and medium-term development plan*, IFLA/FAIFE Report No. 1, Copenhagen, Joint UNESCO, Council of Europe and International Federation of Library Associations/Freedom of Access to Information and Freedom of Information, Kosovo Library Mission.

Garen, M. and Carlton, M.-H. (2005) *An American Hostage*, New York, NY, Simon & Schuster.

Gavidia, J. (2001) Vulnerability Reduction: from knowledge to action. In *World Conference on Natural Disasters, 5–7 February 2001. Preprints*, Kobe, Japan, Japanese Government.

Gergana, A. (2001) *Perspective on Managing Cultural Heritage during Protracted Conflicts: with specific reference to the post-Oslo period in Palestine*, MA thesis, University of York, Post-war Reconstruction and Development Unit (unpublished).

Ghaidan, U. and Paolini, A. (2003) A Short History of the Iraq National Museum, *Museum International*, **55** (3-4), 97-102.

Gibson, M. (2003) From the Prevention Measures to the Fact-finding Mission, *Museum International*, **55** (3-4), 108-18.

Grissmann, C. (2003) The Inventory of the Kabul Museum: attempts at restoring order, Museum International, **55** (3-4), 71-6.

Herscher, A. and Riedlmayer, A. (2000) Architectural Heritage in Kosovo: a postwar report, *Bosnia Report*, New Series 19/20 (October-December), 38-41.

Hitchcock, A. (2003) Through the Fog of War in Iraq: lessons learned in heritage preservation, *The George Wright Forum*, **20** (4), 28-40.

Human Security Centre (2005) *Human Security Report 2005: war and peace in the 21st century*, Vancouver, University of British Columbia.

International Audit Commission (2004) *Report on Babylon: current condition from 11-13 December 2004*, www.msz.gov.pl/BABILON,REPORT,2200.html?PHPSESSID=3efa046944 40fe6b520c5a08a236d56d [accessed 14 December, 2005].

International Bureau of the Court of Arbitration (2004) *Resolution of Cultural Property Disputes*, 7, Peace Palace Papers, The Hague, Kluwer Law International.

Iraqi Jewish Archive (2003) *Preservation Report 2 October*, Oriental Institute, http://oi.uchicago.edu/OI/IRAQ/mela/IraqiJewishArchiveReport.htm [accessed 10 February 2006].

Jackson, B. and Stepniak, W. (2000) *General Assessment of the Situation of Archives in Kosovo*, Technical Report RP/1998-1999/IV.2.2, Paris, UNESCO.

Johnson, I. M. (2005) The Impact on Libraries and Archives in Iraq of War and Looting in 2003: a preliminary assessment of the damage and subsequent reconstruction efforts, *The International Information & Library Review*, **37** (3), 145-272.

Jordan Times (2004) Jordan Urges Closer Co-operation to Stop Smuggling of Iraqi Treasures, *Jordan Times*, (2 June), www.jordanembassyus.org/06022004007.htm [accessed 8 March 2006].

Kundera, M. (1981) *The Book of Laughter and Forgetting*, New York, Knopf.

Lebanese National Library Rehabilitation Project (n.d.), www.bnlb.org/ [accessed 6 February 2006].

Levin, J. (1992) Cultural Heritage under Fire, *The Getty Conservation Newsletter*, **7.1** (Spring), www.getty.edu/conservation/publications/newsletters/7_1/cultural.html [accessed 8 March 2006].

Lufkin, M. (2004) Saddam's Secret Hoard of Jewish Manuscripts, *Art Newspaper*, 1 (12 January).

Maass, P. (1999) Cultural Property and Historical Monuments. In Gutman, R. and Rieff, D. (eds), *Crimes of War: what the public should know*, New York, W. W. Norton & Company.

MacKenzie, G. (1996) *General Assessment of the Situation of Archives in Bosnia and Herzegovina*, Paris, UNESCO.

Malloch Brown, M. (2003) Rebuilding Peace: the development dimensions of crisis and post-conflict management, speech at the *Second Committee of the 58th Session of the UN General Assembly at New York, 4 November*, www.undp.org/dpa/statements/erd.html [accessed 26 October 2005].

Marshall, M. G. and Gurr, T. R. (2005) *Peace and Conflict 2005: a global survey of armed conflicts, self-determination movements, and democracy*, Baltimore, MD, College Park, Center for International Development & Conflict Management, University of Maryland.

Müller, H. (2005) Als Irak asperges exporteerde zaten we er niet. Interview. Na 30 jaar oorlogsverslaggeving in het Midden-Oosten is Robert Fisk somber over de toekomst, *De Volkskrant* (8 November), 6.

Omland, A. and Prescott, C. (2002) Afghanistan's Cultural Heritage in Norwegian museums?, *Culture without Context*, 11 (Autumn), 4-7.

Pharès, J. (2003) The National Museum of Lebanon in Beirut, *Museum International*, 55 (3-4), 38-43.

Prescott, C. and Omland, A. (2003), The Schoyen Collection in Norway: demand for the return of objects and questions about Iraq, *Culture without Context*, 13 (Autumn), 8-11.

Presser, J. (1965) *De Ondergang: de vervolging en verdelging van het Nederlandse Jodendom, 1940-1945*, Gravenhage, Staatsuitgeverij.

Recknagel, C. (2002) *Afghanistan: art finds refuge in Switzerland while awaiting return home*, Radio Free Europe, 23 April, www.rferl.org/features/2002/04/23042002055653.asp [accessed 13 February 2006].

Riedlmayer, A. (1995) Libraries Are Not for Burning: international librarianship and the recovery of the destroyed heritage of Bosnia and Herzegovina, *61st IFLA general conference proceedings, 20-25 August*, www.ifla.org/IV/ifla61/61-riea.htm [accessed 8 March 2006].

Riedlmayer, A. (2000a) Libraries and Archives in Kosova: a postwar report, *Bosnia Report*, New Series, **13/14** (December 1999–February 2000), 19–21.

Riedlmayer, A. (2000b) Museums in Kosovo: a first postwar assessment, *Bosnia Report*, New Series, **15/16** (March–June), 27–30.

Schwarz, G. (2005) An Insider's Account of the Evacuation of Babylon, *The Art Newspaper*, (online edition), (7 May), www.library.yale.edu/international/documents/The%20Art%20Newspaper-Teijgeler.htm [accessed 12 December 2005].

Stovel, H. (1998) Risk Preparedness: a management manual for world cultural heritage, Rome, International Centre for the Study of the Preservation and Restoration of Cultural Property (ICCROM).

Teygeler, R. (2005) 'So Yesterday was the Burning of Books': wartime in Iraq, Lecture at *Responsible Stewardship towards Cultural Heritage Materials, Preconference of the IFLA Rare Book and Manuscript Section, Copenhagen, 11 August*, The Iraqi War and Archaeology, a joint Documentation and Information Project by Archaeos Inc. and the Institute of Oriental Studies, University of Vienna, www.archaeos.org/iwa/teijgeler.html [accessed 10 February 2006].

Teijgeler, R. (2001) *Preservation of Archives in Tropical Climates: an annotated bibliography*, Paris/The Hague/Jakarta, International Council on Archives/Algemeen Rijksarchief/National Archives of the Republic of Indonesia, www.knaw.nl/ecpa/grip/publications.html.

Toman, J. (1996) *The Protection of Cultural Property in the Event of Armed Conflict*, Aldershot/Paris, Dartmouth/UNESCO.

United Nations Independent Inquiry Committee into the United Nations Oil-For-Food Programme (2005) *Manipulation of the Oil-For-Food Programme by the Iraqi Regime: oil transactions and illicit payments, humanitarian goods transactions and illicit payments, the escrow bank and the inspection companies, other UN related issues*, New York, United Nations Independent Inquiry Committee, www.iic-offp.org/documents/IIC%20Final%20Report%2027Oct2005.pdf [accessed 14 February 2006].

van der Hoeven, H. and Albada, J. (1996) *Memory of the World. Lost memory: libraries and archives destroyed in the twentieth century*, Paris, UNESCO.

Villelabeitia, I. (2005) Jordan Leads Hunt for Iraq's Looted Treasures, *Reuters AlertNet*, (16 June), www.alertnet.org/ [accessed 13 February 2006].

Whalen, T. P. (2001) A note by the director, *GCI Newsletters*, **16** (2), www.getty.edu/conservation/publications/newsletters/16_2/ notedirector.html [accessed 8 March 2006].

# CHAPTER 10

# Access and the social contract in memory institutions

Helen Forde

## Introduction

This chapter charts some of the changes that are currently taking place in the provision of access to information, and highlights the need to ensure that new methods of access do not ignore the need to ensure access for future generations as well as the present. Much of the current attention to access represents improvements in the absolute right to information, but there is a danger that good preservation management, particularly in the electronic world, is ignored. These improvements include: the absolute right to information; the obligation to enable information retrieval; the requirement that publicly funded and government-funded projects should facilitate access; the growing issues surrounding electronic access and the real needs of the end-user; the social agenda for access to information; and the importance of making the end-user comfortable with accessing information, be it in a traditional or virtual format.

## Access and the social contract in publicly funded institutions

In considering these issues some definitions and parameters would not go amiss. Access to information is perhaps the simplest of the concepts, but putting that together with 'the social contract' and 'publicly funded institutions' brings in more complex issues. Rousseau's proposition of the equality of all relates in this instance to the right of access to information for all, equally – this is an inalienable right. The role of publicly funded institutions, the memory institutions of the chapter title, is to respond to that inalienable right. I would argue further that the provision of public resources (i.e., resources owned by all in Rousseau's terms) to libraries, museums and archives (defined as memory institutions) confers a social as well as a moral obligation on them to facilitate access to the information they hold, and that this contract is only slowly being recognized by both sides. Memory institutions have, for many years, collected, preserved and made material available, but often on their own terms; the priorities have frequently been those of the organization rather than those of the public. Curators, archivists and librarians have had the content and care of collections at the central core of their responsibilities, stressing the academic and holistic qualities of their holdings, acting in some cases as fortresses into which only the brave dared venture. For their part, individuals have often been slow (or afraid) to assert their right to the information thus held, or they may simply not know that the information exists. This chapter charts some of the changes that are currently taking place, suggests some of the ways in which the social contract must be carried out and argues that a balance is needed between access and preservation in memory institutions, to ensure that the contract with present users is extended to future users as well.

## Absolute right to information

Access to information has become a political issue in recent years; not that it has ever been far from that agenda, but it has frequently been more in terms of denying access to citizens than empowering them to demand their rights. Attempts to prevent information from falling into the wrong hands have been - and in some cases still are - a major plank in the policy of any oppressive regime over the centuries. Examples abound, from the papers burnt during the French Revolution, through the problems experienced in unifying the two parts of Germany after the fall of the Berlin wall in 1989, to more recent efforts by Saddam Hussein's regime in Iraq. Information is power, as all regimes are aware.

## Freedom of Information Acts

Human rights issues for individuals, propelled into the public arena by global reporting systems and instant access to current affairs on radio and television, have, however, become more prominent lately, signalled by the increasing number of Freedom of Information Acts. Pioneered by the USA in 1966, such Acts are now common in many parts of the world, one of the most recent being the draft Bill agreed by the ruling coalition in Germany in December 2004. There, the principle of official secrecy is to be converted into a general right to access to files for the public. Paragraph 1 of the draft Bill declares: 'In accordance with this Act, every person has the right with respect to the authorities of the Federal Government of the Federal Republic of Germany of access to official items of information without being obliged to demonstrate a legal interest in the same.' By way of an explanation it says 'access to information and transparency with regard to the decisions reached by public authorities are important preconditions for the effective exercising of civil rights' (Smith, R., 2004). The Truth and Reconciliation Commissions in South Africa, in parts of Latin America, in several countries in Eastern Europe and in the former countries of the USSR have been a powerful influence on these developments. In many cases they have changed the definition of archives from official documents, which chart the development of an organization, to include all available evidence, in whatever format, and they have demonstrated the power of ordinary people to assert their rights. Not that all such attempts at extending democratic rights have been successful; many questions and technical problems remain, such as those demonstrated in Rwanda, where the Commission is dealing with a multitude of problems, including language difficulties, and the complexities of presenting multifarious evidence from different parts of the world to the International Court at the Hague. Some former Communist regimes have been slow to follow the general trend towards open information, and even now the culture of access for all is not widely recognized in parts of the world where information was ever only accessed by an elite. Efforts to extend access must continue, through demonstration of the benefits and international pressure. This is the essential, basic belief, which must then be followed by the more sophisticated concept of the social contract between public money and memory institutions. Much of the foregoing relates to archives, but other memory institutions are involved too, especially museums, where repatriation of material to native populations – frequently initiated as a result of new access to information – has become a significant issue in the past few years.

Not surprisingly, the preservation of such material is fraught with difficulties: which individual or organization has the responsibility to ensure its survival? Will it be kept under adequate conditions in organizations which, understandably, are wholly pre-occupied with the immediate plight of refugees? Will it be secure in the care of state organizations, even memory institutions, which may be tainted due to associations with a repressive regime? How can professionals be brought in to help if funds are limited in the extreme? These questions all crop up in the context of preserving the evidence of identity and human rights, adding a previously unacknowledged dimension to the efforts of those involved.

## Obligation to enable information retrieval

Public institutions, in all countries where Freedom of Information Acts have been passed, have an obligation to comply with requirements which include not only making material available, but also providing the means to find it. Inability to discover the information required because of a lack of catalogues, documentation or indexes is not an acceptable reason for failing to provide the information. Consequently, in the UK at least, the effects of many years of underfunding for core activities in memory institutions, such as library and archive cataloguing or museum documentation, are now becoming apparent, not least because of the increasing ubiquity of online resources. The backlogs are significant, but are now becoming priorities in the 'information age' dominated by targets and annual plans. Considerable efforts are being made, with welcome acknowledgement that the provision of adequate means of identification and description is a core requirement. The penalties associated with an inability to find required information are beginning to loom large. The slow march of standardization of descriptive terminology across the three domains is still in its infancy, but the mere fact that it is being discussed is witness to a realization – that the users of memory material are rarely concerned about the location of their required information – what they want is the actual information in an accessible and compatible format. Good cataloguing, especially if it is online, offers that to them. User expectation has risen, driving up standards and forcing organizations to reconsider their priorities. Cataloguing is also a major factor in the preservation of material, since it identifies it and its location, avoiding unnecessary and possibly damaging handling of artefacts, obviating the random search as well as offering an opportunity to assess the preservation status of items.

Records management too has recently received welcome attention from organizations which, apparently, previously paid scant attention to the importance of ensuring speedy retrieval of current records created and held by them. The number of posts created in Government departments, agencies and police forces for records managers in the UK over the past few years, for example, is a significant admission of the need to improve accountability and transparency, together with the growing realization of the importance of employing trained professionals to achieve the results required by Government.

## Access to information required by public funders of projects

Access to information is also, increasingly, one of the requirements for funding public projects in the UK. The public supports the Heritage Lottery Fund (n.d.), which has become one of the major sources of funding for a large number of memory institution projects. It specifies that it supports projects 'which aim to make sure everyone can learn about, have access to and enjoy their heritage'. In this case, that is heritage information, but it can also be crucial information for individuals, such as pension or property rights. Substantial lottery resources have also been allocated to develop archive networks across the UK, such as Access to Archives (A2A), the Scottish Archives Network (SCAN), Archives Network Wales and the Archives Hub, the university network (a national gateway to descriptions of archives in UK universities and colleges). These grants, primarily for improved access, nevertheless also contribute to the freedom of information (FOI) goal of enabling information retrieval.

Government support has also been forthcoming for innovative projects involving access to information in cross-domain projects, such as Moving Here (www.movinghere.org.uk/), an electronic project seeking to package together sources from museums, libraries and archives on immigration to the UK, and making clear the importance attached to access to information about origins. There are 30 partners currently engaged on the project, having contributed over 200,000 digitized items, and the next phase has just been funded. Other examples are partnership projects such as the People's Network, a programme sponsored by Microsoft and the UK Department for Culture, Media and Sport (DCMS) and carried out by the Museums, Libraries and Archives Council (MLA). This enables all public libraries to offer free internet access to users, attracting new users and providing innovative services via 32,000 computer terminals across 4,200 libraries. An MLA press release noted that in 2004 visits to public libraries had increased by 14 million (Museums, Libraries and Archives Council, 2005a). For the museums, Renaissance in the Regions is the latest DCMS funded MLA programme to develop regional museum hubs/centres of excellence in England, with an emphasis on making information available from the hidden resources of museums all over the country.

## Electronic access to information

All over the world, increasing importance is being given to electronic means of access to information. It forms part of almost every Government agenda, whether central, regional or local. Achieving results is difficult, in both providing information that is useful and accessible for the citizen and making it technologically accessible to all. Ensuring that all parts of the information platform are connected is equally difficult, hence the aspiration of joined-up government has so far produced very patchy results. In memory institutions the results are equally patchy – it is hardly surprising, given the sheer volume of material on offer. Access, however, is improving and the scale of digitization projects is increasing as understanding of the complexities – but also the advantages – of spreading information more widely becomes increasingly apparent. The future Google partnership project with the major university libraries of Oxford, Stanford, Michigan and Harvard and the New York Public Library, announced in December 2004, was followed 24 hours later by an agreement by 10 international libraries to add digitized book collections to the Text archive project (Chillingworth, 2004). The latter, a San Francisco-based initiative to give free access to historic collections, already offers a million texts available online. These projects are indicative of the scaling-up of aspirations, dwarfing earlier projects merely concerned with the iconic holdings of individual memory institutions.

To date, most digitization projects, large or small, have confined themselves to their own domains, with few aspiring to cross-domain involvement. The management issues, compatibility issues and the scale of such projects require partnership and involvement of a nature that can only be provided by the larger archives, libraries or museums. The very competitive nature of some of these initiatives, however, suggests that the earlier collection-building tendencies in publicly funded institutions are being replaced by the aspirations of even larger organizations – some of them commercial and therefore with a different agenda – which seek to dominate global information systems. On a smaller scale, a recent survey in the UK (Museums, Libraries and Archives Council, 2005b), significantly entitled *Digital Knowledge for All, but What about for Ever?*, concluded that in selected regions there is a significant commitment to digitization in public memory institutions, but 90% of such projects were externally funded and took no account of the need to provide the long-term sustainable support necessary to ensure access in the future.

## Are access-related projects delivering what is required?

Technical, financial and organizational complexities associated with large projects tend to overshadow many of the real questions which need to be asked. Is access to information really being promoted and, if so, how can the benefits of access be measured? Is digitization meeting the needs of users? Are they just being offered packaged information? Does this inhibit or promote personal discovery? And how can success or failure be measured in terms relating to the requirement to provide information according to the social contract? Clarity is crucial since choices about further projects cannot be made without understanding the benefits flowing from current increased access. The answers are also important in the context of this chapter, given that any increased access necessarily implies the need for preservation.

Some work is going on to help identify the tangible benefits of access to information, but it is not easy, especially in the economic format adopted by governments and funders. A report for the MLA on developing the evidence base for the value of memory institutions (Burns Owens Partnership, 2005) cites the development in the USA of the concept of 'social capital' as the main reason why cultural participation (which the authors equate with the work of memory institutions in the UK) is regarded as beneficial. However, the authors concluded that the accumulated evaluation on this in the UK is sparse. Some work has been done, however, even if it does not follow the American model. A study in 2001 of what libraries were delivering to individuals (Coalter, 2001) identified their role as one which empowered individuals to undertake research for information that is otherwise difficult to access. Other research has been undertaken to evaluate the efficacy of websites as information carriers, notably that of the Moving Here website, which was the subject of a report by the Tavistock Institute in 2004. The evaluation looked at how usable, useful and valuable the project website is, in particular the strengths and weaknesses of the cross-sectoral partnership model. All these, and other reports in different parts of the world, demonstrate that organizations are aware of the need to evaluate impact and value for the end-user, although the criteria for evaluation are not easy to define. It must be built into any project from the beginning and, if done appropriately, enables public institutions to demonstrate that they have used funding to promote access, to learn lessons for improvement in the future, or to develop methodologies and systems to measure success or failure. A recent report on the People's Network noted the importance of measuring the benefits and the development of a toolkit called LONGITUDE (Library Networking Impact Toolkit for a User-driven Environment) to do just that (www.mla.gov.uk).

## Issues raised by electronic dissemination of information

Both major and less grandiose projects uncover further access, and, by definition, preservation difficulties. One of the more ambitious undertakings is COVAX (www.covax.org/primera.htm), the European programme for the dissemination of European cultural heritage using XML.

> COVAX has four basic aims: dissemination of European Culture Heritage, facilitating access for European citizens to primary sources of intellectual, cultural and scientific heritage stored in archives, libraries and museums; exploitation over the Internet of existing cultural infrastructures; the use of standards in the field of information structure and retrieval and interoperability between systems (interoperable access to distributed resources) based on the complementary capabilities of each partner.

At the humbler end of the scale are the aspirations of local organizations to disseminate information about geographical areas. Increasing use of the resources on the internet to access information confuses the issues of ownership and responsibility for maintaining the integrity of that information. 'Ownership of and access to collections are no longer synonymous' (Smith, A., 2004, 3). Electronic copyright has become a big issue, as has the business of selling expertise on the internet, for example in the guise of perfect coursework for students. Who owns what? This is access in ways not envisaged by our predecessors, and the wrinkles need to be smoothed out by dialogue and partnership between memory institutions and commercial publishers. Responsibility for maintaining electronic journals is a particular case in point, where publishers tend to keep them current for only a short time. And yet, it is not so long ago that libraries were desperate to solve the problem of maintaining storage areas crammed to the ceiling with out-of-date serials.

Electronic provision is not quite the panacea that might have been envisaged. Higher education organizations in particular are concerned that the loss of such information will lead to a real gap in research and a failure to use the results of such research in timely and appropriate ways. Where does preservation stand in this?

## Voice of the user and social inclusion

All is not doom and gloom, however. An increasing emphasis has been placed on consultation with users of memory institutions in the last few years to determine their needs. This can be related to the growing perception that such organizations must be responsive and cannot assume understanding of requirements. It is also against a background of increasing insistence that museums, libraries and archives have functions over and above those with which they have been associated traditionally – social, educational, and even health policies cite the value of exploiting historic materials. The importance of culture in the well-being of a nation is a recurrent theme, presenting new opportunities, if also new challenges. One of the latter is engagement with minority groups and even non-users, trying to draw in those who are either averse to the services on offer or feel themselves culturally excluded. Many of the initiatives in this have come from the USA, where programmes for immigrant groups have a long history, but they also stem from other countries with a concern to avoid the exclusion of valuable groups of citizens. If this is part of the social contract which memory institutions have with the public, how have they responded and what are the implications?

## Access opportunities

Virtual access, 24/7, is a growing concept in an electronic age and some memory organizations are now developing partnerships with others around the globe so that they can provide a seamless 24-hour enquiry service by directing electronic enquiries to the appropriate time zone. In the UK, the People's Network recently launched a new 24/7 reference service online, which is described as 'a national effort in contrast to the consortial and institution specific efforts in North America'. It is known as Enquire and, depending on the time of the application, users will be answered by English, American or Canadian librarians working in partnership. These include the UK Museums, Libraries and Archives Council, Co-East, a libraries partnership in the East of England, OCLC Pica, a European co-operative and public library staff in over 50 local authorities (www.libraryjournal.com/index.asp?layout=articlePrint&articleID=CA603 048). Access opportunities on-site are also increasing as more institutions stretch their opening hours either on a regular basis or for special exhibitions or events. While commercial considerations are clearly part of the equation, they nevertheless stimulate innovative ideas for access. The current craze for sleepovers for children in museums is hardly the kind of access envisaged by our predecessors, but appears to be very popular and is probably memorable!

## Development of access through involvement

Encouragement for involvement is a strategy being followed by many such organizations, where the value of participation is perceived as assisting inclusivity as well as contributing to the cultural identity of the geographical area. More research on this has been undertaken in the USA (e.g., the Social Impact of the Arts project at the University of Pennsylvania, see www.ssw.upenn.edu/SIAP/) than in the UK, and there is some way to go to catch up. However, projects such as the development of electronic community archives are now being developed and expanded in various parts of Great Britain. No more than an extension of the age-old fascination with the history of places, people and activities, it stems from a desire to ensure that the history and endeavours of previous generations are not lost. But because such documentation, photographs, maps, oral history clips and many other items can be collected and exhibited electronically to a worldwide audience, the impact is much greater than that of the manuscript parish or community history deposited in a local archive. The added value is in the increased social contact and community involvement. The down-side can be the lack of professional technical input which renders the electronic base unstable and risks the loss of information, raising preservation issues again. Cultural festivals held in museums for immigrant communities offer similar benefits of involvement: in that case with the advantage of encouraging the use of memory institutions by new audiences while widening the horizons of the more traditional users. Both those audiences and others also still respond to time-honoured means of access, not least exhibitions. These remain at the heart of the access agenda for many organizations, enabling access for the casual visitor as well as those who come with a specific interest.

## Role of exhibitions

Display is a major focus of museums in particular, where there is less emphasis on individual research and more on presenting information to visitors. Practical difficulties, such as fragility or size of objects, make this almost inevitable, though a trend is discernible towards a more open approach, concentrating more on other senses, such as touch, feel, and even smell, as in the Jorvik Viking Centre in York. Reserve collections too are being opened up for study, and several major Heritage Lottery Fund grants to museums in the UK have made this a requirement for funding. Both museums and other memory institutions frequently focus on special displays and commemorative events to attract a new public, engage with those who might not have visited for some time and bring items in the collections to the attention of the public and media. One of the major objectives is education, another part of the social contract over access, and one best fulfilled by on-site exhibitions, virtual exhibitions and special programmes (real or on the web) designed for particular age groups. This constitutes a major role for memory institutions, and one which fits well with the requirements of government and other funding organizations. Both children and adults are interested in and intrigued by historical artefacts, documents and books, and catching their imagination is not difficult. The trend towards interpretation of historical events is growing. Random examples include the re-creation by adults of battles of the British Civil War or the rebuilding and interpretation of historic sites where children come by the coach load to dress up and participate. The present enthusiasm for wartime cookery events is another good example, where the educative function of memory institutions of exhibiting volumes of wartime recipes, manuscript notebooks with details of personal recipes, or surviving tins of food available during the war, is combined with a real desire on the part of adults to demonstrate to the current generation of children what life was like under difficult conditions 60 years ago. All are indicative of the level of interest in historic events and places.

Exhibitions and demonstrations also offer an opportunity to educate the public in good stewardship. Reduced light levels when fragile paper, photographic materials or textiles are on display frequently provoke reactions from visitors, and a clear explanation at the entrance of an exhibition introduces issues surrounding the care of the items and often provokes positive comment. In the UK the National Trust offers visitors to some of the properties in its care the opportunity to touch sample fabrics over the course of a season, demonstrating the degree of wear and tear that this produces. It also offers explanations about the research being undertaken on the quantity of dust and dirt brought in through the doors, and the resultant damage. Blue wool test strips are visible in many rooms and guides are encouraged to explain their role in measuring light damage. Each year tickets are sold to the public for involvement in the 'putting to bed' exercise carried out at the end of October in each property when it is closed up for the winter months. Grasping such opportunities to educate the public and staff in basic approaches to preservation is a valuable way of ensuring that the access granted today will still be available for future visitors.

## Ease of access and changing attitudes of organization to visitors

A good working environment might seem a natural requirement for a good relationship between users and the organizations they visit, whether on-site or online. If so, it is one which has rarely been articulated and often ignored. This is not necessarily because the need is not acknowledged, but more often on account of a lack of funds. Museums crammed with objects that are poorly labelled and without context, libraries with rows of dog-eared books exuding little appeal to reluctant readers, and archives with cramped working conditions and reader printers that are always out of order are all too familiar. Concerted efforts to improve these environments are beginning to make a difference. Beyond the physical environment, emphasis is also being laid on the need to welcome and encourage visitors, users, readers and even customers. The vocabulary is changing: 'Front of house' staff, a phrase once associated only with hotels, is now a concept recognized in memory institutions as valid for ensuring that those who visit in person are well looked after and enjoy the experience. The obligation conferred on an organization to treat all visitors equally and offer them the same opportunities, as part of the social contract, has not been lost upon management staff across the world. Websites have made it simpler to advertise opening times, locations and up-to-date information for intending visitors, in the same way that electronic catalogues have made identification of the correct institution to visit much easier. Thus revamped premises combine with electronic information and new concepts about welcoming users to improve the social contract from the point of view of the user and make it easier for the memory institutions to encourage new visitors. Success breeds success.

## The essential role of preservation

All this activity for access underlines the need for preservation management. Publicly funded memory institutions have always fulfilled traditional conservation and preservation roles, though the names of these specialist and curatorial functions change from time to time. The challenges now are greater than they have ever been. More access equals greater handling of fragile materials, greater demand for exhibitions on-site, off-site and virtual, a proliferation of electronic material and increasing reliance on digitization for the dissemination of materials. The care of traditional materials was always fraught, due to the impossibility of ensuring that it all survived, the need to prioritize for spending scarce resources and the decreasing pool of specialists to undertake the work. The electronic challenges are far greater given the fragility of the medium and the commercial pressures for obsolescence of both hardware and software. The legacy being left to our successors is awesome in its complexity and potential cost.

Memory institutions deal with this in different ways. For some it is explicit. For example, in the UK the National Maritime Museum (www.nmm.ac.uk/server/show/nav.005006000) cites stewardship as one of its strategic aims: 'The Museum's responsibilities are to safeguard and enhance the value of its pre-eminent assets.' The British Library's (2001) Strategic Plan states that:

The British Library is responsible for:

- Ensuring the comprehensive coverage, recording and preservation of the UK national published archive
- Ensuring the broad UK coverage and preservation of research material from overseas.                                        (British Library, 2001)

For others, and especially for smaller organizations, it still needs reiteration. Preservation may be implicit in many of the activities undertaken, but to ensure that the need is recognized and planned for, it must be clearly stated – and funded. The danger faced by organizations with huge demands on the material they hold is grinding deterioration through popularity in the current generation, without adequate resources to ensure survival for subsequent generations. The requirement on those holding digital assets is equally demanding and requires significant definition of responsibilities, as well as preservation funding built into any projects where the resulting material requires permanent preservation.

## Conclusion

Everything points to a need to balance the requirements for access to information with appropriate preservation techniques to avoid future gaps in knowledge, particularly for the following generations. Unfortunately, this core requirement is less attractive as an activity than the currently popular provision of access. Projects for access to information are more exciting, show results sooner and fulfil the political agenda. And politicians themselves do not capitalize on preservation issues in libraries, archives and museums, since they rarely produce headlines. The collapse of historic buildings, or the desecration of world heritage sites present fleeting opportunities to raise awareness but all too often these are not related to the equally disastrous loss of information in other formats. The perception of good stewardship is low, given that the proof of successful preservation is prolonged survival, measured in centuries rather than months. Add to this the historic misconception that preservation is against access and a myth has to be overcome as well.

## References

British Library (2001) *Strategic Plan*,
    www.bl.uk/about/collectioncare/activities.html#strategy.
Burns Owens Partnership (2005) *New Directions in Social Policy: developing the evidence base for museums, libraries and archives*, London, Museums, Libraries and Archives Council.
Chillingworth, M. (2004) Internet Archive to Build Alternative to Google,

*Information World Review*, (21 December),
www.iwr.co.uk/information-world-review/news/2083906/
internet-archive-build-alternative-google.

Coalter, F. (2001) *Realising the Potential of Cultural Services: the case for libraries*,
Edinburgh, Centre for Leisure Research at the University of Edinburgh.

Heritage Lottery Fund (n.d.) *Thinking about Access*,
www.hlf.org.uk/NR/rdonlyres/5FE01552-03B1-48C4-986A-
C5309B8B8F5C/0/ThinkingAboutAccess.pdf.

Museums, Libraries and Archives Council (2005a) *Library Use Soars*,
www.literacytrust.org.uk/Database/stats/libstats.html#soars.

Museums, Libraries and Archives Council (2005b) *Digital Knowledge for All,
but What about for Ever?*, www.mla.gov.uk.

Smith, A. (2004) Mapping the Preservation Landscape. In *Access in the Future
Tense*, Washington DC, Council on Library and Information Resources,
www.clir.org/pubs/reports/pub126/smith1.html.

Smith, R. (2004) Germany's Ruling Coalition Gets Serious about Freedom of
Information, *Heise*, (15 December),
www.heise.de/english/newsticker/news/54286.

# CHAPTER 11

# Redefining 'the collection' in the 21st century

## G. E. Gorman and Sydney J. Shep

## Introduction

The development of preservation management strategies across a range of media forms has resulted in a reassessment of the nature and role of the collection. This chapter reviews the development of interest in preservation management and discusses current thinking on collection development and management in light of the, at times, conflicting needs of preservation and access, and as a result of digitization activity across the museum, library and archive sectors.

## Primary emphasis on building collections

While preservation and the management of preservation activities have played a role in heritage institutions - libraries, archives and museums - throughout history, this role has ranged from passive to proactive. As far as we can determine, early libraries and archives existed to collect and protect heritage resources, but the protection was often an afterthought or side effect of the collecting urge. That is, these institutions saw their role primarily as custodians of materials, protecting them from the hoi polloi and from the vandals of the day.

This custodial function was essentially reactionary - keeping people and the elements away from whatever was in the collection. The great collections of the 18th and 19th centuries (the British Museum and the Bibliothèque Nationale are good examples) were primarily magnets for artefacts, which were stored and largely ignored. The story of the world's great libraries is primarily a story of collection building, and until perhaps the mid-20th century this is what libraries did: collected, processed and stored. And in libraries this was the term used: 'collection building'. Whether we look at archives, libraries or museums, the urge to build seems to have been paramount until comparatively recently.

In the library world the emphasis on building began to wane after World War 2 and was gradually replaced by a more measured, 'scientific' approach that became known as collection development. This was an era in which collections were tailored more closely to their client base, and various benchmarking criteria were introduced, including Conspectus. Most recently collection development has given way to collection management, in which a more holistic approach is taken to how we collect, process, store, use, evaluate and *preserve* the intellectual heritage found in libraries. This evolution reflects what Gorman and Miller (1997, x) have called 'a subtle paradigmatic shift both from discrete institutional collections to a wider library world and from narrower issues specific to collection building to a rather daunting range of issues drawn from the wider aspects of professional practice. In broad terms these issues encompass ... a process of information gathering, communication co-ordination, policy formulation, evaluation and planning'.

Preservation has always been a sub-theme in collection building and collection development, but existed somewhere outside the mainstream activity of building and developing. It was not until collection management became the norm that preservation was brought in from the cold, as it were.

## The development of preservation as a systematic activity

This is not to say that preservation was not a concern in the heady days of collection building; rather, it was somewhat *ad hoc* and taken seriously by relatively small numbers of professionals. Higginbotham's excellent treatise on early preservation activities in American libraries, *Our Past Preserved: a history of American library preservation, 1876–1910*, records many of these early concerns: poor paper quality, deteriorating bindings, and problems caused by damp, fire, poor storage conditions and chemicals in the fumes from gas used for lighting. This list is almost endless, and

Higginbotham recounts the various individual attempts to deal with one or more of these at a local level. Very rarely did these *ad hoc* activities go beyond the walls of a particular institution. One exception recounted by Higginbotham (1990, 19) was at the 1877 Conference of Librarians in London, where Guillaume Depping suggested that a committee of librarians and chemists be formed to investigate the causes of leather deterioration. However not much seems to have come of this suggestion.

So, well into the 20th century the treatment of preservation issues was rather like fire fighting - putting out spot fires as they occurred here and there. Why was this so? The answer lies, according to Henderson's plausible observations, in the rapid growth of collections and the number of libraries following the end of World War 2. We are well enough aware of the 'information explosion', so this does not require reiterating here except to say that this lay behind the almost obsessive emphasis on collection building as noted above - publications were appearing like confetti, and funds were almost as plentiful. This was accompanied by the expansion of the library sector, which meant that more books were being purchased, and national collections were expanding. In the UK, for example, we saw the development of the 'new' universities (Sussex, Kent, East Anglia, etc.); in Australia and New Zealand the colleges of advanced education and polytechnics respectively; and in the US the expansion of publicly funded universities, with the New York and California systems as prime examples. Development was so rapid, in other words, that the information professional had little time to consider the preservation needs of what was regarded as an insignificant percentage of their overall collections. As Henderson (1996, 276) puts it,

> This growth masked at least somewhat the effect of the aging of older materials. Librarians were preoccupied by the increase in the size of their collections fostered by the need to keep up with growing user populations, burgeoning staffs, emerging disciplines, and space to accommodate it all. In addition the rapidly expanding population and growing economy seemed to promise unending growth and expansion for academic, public and other libraries of all types.

## Preservation comes of age

One cannot put a precise date on when collection development became collection management, and likewise one cannot specify that moment when preservation became a mainstream concern of information managers, conservators and archivists. As McDonald (1990, 484) remarks, 'few fields emerge full-blown. ... Preservation, a field inherently concerned with the cultural production of the past, is largely and ironically unaware of its own history'. What we do know is that preservation as the concern for specific artefacts and documents continued to be the norm into the 1960s at least. In the US 1964 seems to have been a watershed year, with the publication of the Williams Report, which recommended a national preservation collection of books to be maintained under federal government control (Williams, 1964). While the recommendations of Williams never came to fruition, it is generally recognized that his work alerted the community to the need to perceive preservation as something applicable to entire collections, and indeed the national cultural heritage as represented in libraries. This represented a major shift in thinking, and has been the principle behind the rapid development of preservation protocols, procedures and research in recent decades.

The momentum for co-ordinated, planned and integrated preservation management seems to have occurred, in the West at least, in the 1980s. The statement by Brown University (2002) of its own preservation management evolution stands as a good example of this development. Example 11.1, condensed from the Brown University Library website, shows how preservation evolved from a primary concern with exceptional materials (books and manuscripts with special content or binding) to broad concern with the full range of recorded information owned by this particular library. Further, it goes beyond this to exhibit a strong future orientation in its proactive stance regarding disaster planning, new technologies and other evolving aspects of preservation management.

## Where are we today?

When one thinks of preservation in the documentary heritage sector, probably the first issue that comes to mind is that of acidic paper, which is generally estimated to affect approximately 80% of a typical collection.

## Example 11.1

### The development of preservation activities at Brown University, Rhode Island

The Preservation Department at the Brown University Library is responsible for protecting and maintaining all the materials owned by the library and for *preserving their intellectual content and physical structure*. Both the content and package are regarded as worthy of preservation.

Originally preservation was a rather *ad hoc* process, focusing primarily on the care of old, fragile and historically interesting materials. That is, preservation was highly selective. In general the focal point for these early preservation efforts was the conservation techniques which required the skills of highly trained book binders and paper conservators.

Modern preservation activities at Brown University Library began with the report of the Preservation Coordinating Committee, which produced a Preservation Plan for Brown Libraries in 1983. This Plan was not fully implemented until 1987, which also saw the creation of a central planning facility for preservation and which resulted in the April 1989 publication, *Recommendations for a Preservation Program at Brown University Library*. The report outlined an expanded preservation program for the Library and was implemented in early 1993, with the establishment of a new Preservation Department and appointment of a department head.

Now preservation efforts have been expanded to include *all library materials, in all formats*. As noted in the various reports on preservation at Brown University Library issued in the 1980s, the general collections are in considerable danger because of their *poor quality paper content*, because of *high use, environmental control instability*, and *ever increasing space and storage pressures*.

The Preservation Department assists in meeting the needs of the general collections, while continuing efforts are focused on Special Collections. The Preservation Department at Brown University Library consists of the following components:

(1)  the Bindery Unit, which has responsibility for all aspects of commercial binding as well as for *mending and repair* of the circulating collection, labelling, marking, and final *processing of all*

*newly received books*, and *construction of archival enclosures* for damaged, at risk, and brittle books;
(2) the Conservation Unit, which works with varied materials from this special collections library providing *expertise and specialized techniques to maintain the material in its original state*;
(3) NEH Preservation, funded by an endowment established with the help of a National Endowment of the Humanities award;
(4) the Collection Storage and Care Unit, with responsibility for *stacks maintenance*.

The functions of the Brown University Library Preservation Department are as follows:

- End processing of newly acquired materials
- Commercial binding
- Repair of circulating materials
- Care and treatment of special collections
- Environmental monitoring
- Disaster and emergency planning and response
- Staff and user education programmes
- Investigating new preservation technologies
- Storage coordination.

(Condensed from www.brown.edu/Facilities/University_Library/
Preservation/Preservation.html)

While the use of acidic paper all but ceased in the developed world by the 1960s, this is not the case in developing countries, which continue to use cheaper, easily produced paper with high acid content: it is thus a continuing problem. Whether a book was produced in the early 20th century in the West or yesterday in a developing country, the reality is that untreated acidic paper results in the phenomenon we call 'brittle books': books in such a weakened state that their use is often prohibited. The problem of brittle books is the motivation behind the growing awareness of the need for proactive preservation management that, in the early years of the 21st century, has clearly become a priority in any repository that takes its mission seriously.

The principal means of dealing with brittle books are a history of the modern techniques of collection management. All of these techniques have to do with the reformatting of materials to make them, or rather their surrogates, usable once again. It started with microfilm in the 1930s (and, somewhat later, microfiche) – a simple, cost-effective and low technology means of transferring content from one medium to another, albeit a medium not much loved by users of these materials.

With the advent of digital technology, there is a growing move from microform to optical disk, and it is now known that microform materials are easily transferred to disk. At the same time, however, we are uncertain of the stability of optical disk technology, and of its viability in terms of long-term storage and retrieval, so it is likely that hybrid systems – microform and optical disks – will be the order of the day for some time to come.

Despite advances in digital technology and the application of text encoding software, experts are still uncertain as to the effects of media obsolescence on current technologies, so the issue of ease of migration of these technologies is of considerable concern. Not only that, but also the manpower and financial costs involved in migration seem to cause considerable unease among managers. There is, then, still much to be learned about how we deal with the issue of brittle books, and this is only one aspect of present-day preservation management.

A related process is that of direct optical disk scanning – texts scanned directly into digital form and stored in an automated retrieval system – as distinct from texts that are migrated from one technology (microform) to another (optical disk). The benefits of digital scanning are obvious: the saving of time and money, the provision of immediate access to a multitude of users at any time and in any place, the massive storage capacity of most systems, and the reduction in manpower needed to manage text storage and retrieval.

Alongside the emergence of new technologies for text imaging and electronic storage and retrieval there is an underlying and continuing interest in learning how better to stabilize materials in their original formats. For many years, especially in the archives community, professionals have experimented with a variety of methods of controlling the light, temperature and humidity that affects print material containers (including paper and binding). The literature on archival containers is myriad and mysterious to the non-expert, with everything from acid-free plastics to freeze-drying being tried at one time or another (Henderson, 1996). How to control the total climate (temperature, humidity, air movement, UV radiation, etc.) in which materials are housed continues to exercise preservation managers, engineers and architects; this is unlikely to change in the near future, or as long as hybrid preservation continues to be a reality.

As the Brown University experts state, an unrealistic option is to wait and do nothing. ... '[W]e in the preservation field have seen the consequences of inaction: books which literally are flaking away, pages which cannot be lifted to turn without tearing, parts of text lost forever so that even complete reformatting is impossible' (www.brown.edu/ Facilities/University_Library/Preservation/Preservation.html).

## New media and new collections

It is precisely in recognition of this sentiment that the preservation potential, as well as the as yet unrecognized problems, of the new media are coming to the forefront of preservation management thinking. The central role of preservation management in contemporary collection management policy and practice can be attributed, in part, to the twin imperatives of technology and digitization. In 2001 and again in 2004, the American-based Institute of Museum and Library Services (IMLS) surveyed five types of institution – museums, public libraries, academic libraries, archives and state library administrative agencies – to determine the status of new technology adoption and digitization activities. A comparison of digitization goals across sectors and across time reveals a fundamental shift in focus. Each sector was asked to nominate their top three reasons for digitization activities from a list of 17 possibilities; data was collated, expressed as a percentage, ranked, then compared between 2001 and 2004. Archives were omitted from the 2001 census, and only their digitization activities and priorities were included in 2004. Table 11.1 synthesizes the individual sector data provided in the IMLS report.

**Table 11.1**    Top three goals for digitization activities, 2001 and 2004 (IMLS, 2005)

| Rationale for digitization activities | Museums [n= 479] 2001, % | 2004, % | Public libraries [n= 239] 2001, % | 2004, % | Academic libraries [n= 70] 2001, % | 2004, % | State library admin agencies [n= 42] 2001, % | 2004, % |
|---|---|---|---|---|---|---|---|---|
| Minimize damage to original materials | 32.6 | 33.0 | | 23.2 | 35.2 | | 40.5 | |
| Preserve materials of importance and value | 31.3 | 48.7 | 37.4 | 42.2 | 40.8 | 34.9 | 35.1 | 50.0 |
| Increase access to collections/materials/ files | | 56.0 | | 32.2 | | 42.9 | | 87.5 |
| Increase interest in institution | | | 32.5 | | 31.0 | | 43.2 | |
| Provide access to materials via the web | | | 26.7 | | | 36.5 | | 72.5 |
| Don't know/not applicable | 27.9 | | | | | | | |

Broadly speaking, these figures demonstrate several trends: a shift away from electronically marketing the institution to a predominant concern with public access to materials; a shift away from physical and preventative conservation of originals to targeted preservation of culturally and economically important assets; and finally, a shift from targeted preservation to increased public access. These trends confirm a greater awareness of the importance of specific collection items as well as the need to make these items available for viewing and use.

Interestingly, however, although access is a driver, three-quarters of the institutions do not engage in user needs assessments in relation to their digital collections, and less than half have robust digitization policies. As a result, IMLS is now supporting targeted research into users and their needs, how people use electronic information, systems design issues related to users and usability, and the nexus of knowledge integration, preservation and the integration of digital and physical experiences (Ray, 2004).

The focus on access dovetails with the tenets of the new museology and its convergence with heritage preservation (Vinson, 2001). Traditional models of collecting and connoisseurship which fostered the cultural hegemony of the state and its elites have been deconstructed by physical and virtual heritage institutions in the process of exploring issues of community and identity using a far broader range of artefactual records in settings which promote interactivity, entertainment and new visual literacies (Halpin, 1997). Local concerns, revisionist histories and the profiling of minority groups and interests are now themes of choice as curators and exhibition designers investigate new imaginings of and storytelling narratives for their publics.

At the same time, the notion of the collection itself as a static and fixed assemblage of items housed in a single institution in perpetuity has been redefined. Distributed collections with multiple custodial and guardianship roles and rights, particularly for archives and indigenous cultural property, are joined by travelling collections temporarily housed in flexible spaces, and virtual collections of digitized surrogates which erase geopolitical as well as institutional boundaries. The establishment of collaborative networks such as the British-based Museums, Libraries and Archives Council (MLA) emphasize cross-domain collaboration among institutions in the cultural heritage sector. While the aim is to facilitate seamless, networked access to collections, an integrated stewardship strategy underwritten by sound preservation management principles brings together domains that have hitherto operated in isolation and with little recognition or appreciation of essential commonalities and constructive differences. As Matthews and Thebridge (2001) note, continuity, culture and competition are now joined by co-operation, collaboration and co-ordination.

As many commentators remark, however, the digital imperative has called into question both the status of the artefact and the contexts in which it is placed (CLIR, 2001). Mined for content, aggregated collections must be combined with metadata harvesting to ensure that the context(s) of creation and transmission as well as provenance are tagged to individual items. Various user groups demand different levels of informational detail, so what serves one user for its illustrative value will rarely satisfy an academic researcher whose selection of a surrogate over an original requires value-added features (Ray, 2004). Unlimited access can collide with cultural sensitivities and intellectual property rights, and run counter to calls for artefactual repatriation.

Even the concept of history itself is being rewritten. Jaqueline Spence argues that

> ...technological advance means that history need no longer be defined by the history of political power, but rather by what we choose to preserve in terms of electronic data, documentation, and records ... We should be considering the preservation of our history over centuries, perhaps even millennia. This will mean developing new ways of thinking about how cumulative histories are gathered, stored, and protected, preparing for even more revolutionary forms of document and historical narrative, and taking a really long-term and holistic view.                                          (Spence, 2005, 366, 375)

She extends the notion of social inclusion beyond passive consumption to a collective responsibility, where the preservation process starts at the moment of creation, and by those who created the records in the first place: 'the idea being proposed here is to create a chain of responsibility that follows the chain of custody' (Spence, 2005, 376).

Paul Gherman elaborates on this concept by opening up the debate on the increasing obsolescence of academic and research libraries in the wake of digitized, licensed and web-based collections as well as new media and born-digital materials. He reconfigures the notion of institutional repositories as 'edge' collections: that is, those which emphasize the 'up-stream' collection, preservation and management of dynamic research content rather than the usual 'down-stream' result of scholarly activity in published form.

> Edge collections are those materials that are not part of the scholarly or commercial publishing industry, and often they can be transitory, ephemeral but part of the cultural heritage of a society.... Edge collections can be significant collections of scientific or scholarly findings, or deep and operable collections of cultural heritage materials.                              (Gherman, 2005, 26, 34)

And without society having denominated 'any institutions with the specific role of managing and preserving new forms of cultural heritage in the digital age' (Gherman, 2005, 24), he further suggests that libraries need to reinvent themselves to enable both new forms of collection development and new patterns of scholarship.

## Conclusion

Under the influence of collaborative networks such as MLA and IMLS and new collection and collecting paradigms, it may be that the cultural heritage institution of tomorrow will not be the library, the archive or the museum. Instead, a new, hybrid species of co-ordinated collection activity driven by preservation management principles will shape both physical and virtual cultural heritage institutions of the future.

It is equally likely that technologies and formats as yet not even conceptualized will contribute dramatically to the reshaping of our heritage institutions. But what seems to be emerging is a long-term constant of growing demands for rapid, simple access; the continuing debate will be how to balance this with the need for effective preservation measures, experimenting with a variety of technologies and collaborative arrangements on a global scale.

## References

Brown University Library (2002) Preservation Department,
    www.brown.edu/Facilities/University_Library/Preservation/Preservation.
    html [accessed 1 March 2006].

Council on Library and Information Resources (2001) *The Evidence in Hand: Report of the Task Force on the Artifact in Library Collections*,
    www.clir.org/pubs/pubs.html [accessed 30 March 2006].

Gherman, P. M. (2005) Collecting at the Edge: transforming scholarship,
    *Journal of Library Administration*, **42** (2), 23-34.

Gorman, G. E. and Miller, R. H. (eds) (1997) *Collection Management for the 21st Century*, Westport, CT, Greenwood Press.

Halpin, M. M. (1997) 'Play It Again, Sam': reflections on a new museology,
    *Museum International*, **49** (2), 52-6.

Henderson, W. T. (1996) Preservation: A Quarter Century of Growth. In
    Smith, L.C. and Carter, R. C. (eds), *Technical Services Management, 1965-1990: a quarter century of change and a look to the future. Festschrift for Kathryn Luther Henderson*, Binghamton, NY, Haworth Press, 275-90.

Higginbotham, B. B. (1990) *Our Past Preserved: a history of American library preservation, 1876-1910*, Boston, MA, G. K. Hall.

Institute of Museum and Library Services (2005) *Status of Technology and Digitization in the Nation's Museums and Libraries*, www.imls.gov/publications/TechDig05/index.htm [accessed 30 March 2006].

Matthews, G., and Thebridge, S. (2001) Preservation Management Training and Education: developing a sector-wide approach, *New Library World*, **102** (11-12), 443-51.

McDonald, L. (1990) Forgotten Forebears: concerns with preservation, 1876 to World War I [Bibliographical Essay], *Libraries & Culture*, **25** (4), 483-95.

Ray, J. (2004) Connecting People and Resources: digital programs at the Institute of Museum and Library Services, *Library Hi Tech*, **22** (3), 249-53.

Spence, J. (2005) Small Organizations and Cultural Institutions: a digital future?, *Program: Electronic Library and Information Systems*, **39** (4), 366-80.

Vinson, I. (2001) Heritage and Museology: a new convergence, *Museum International*, **53** (3), 58-64.

Williams, G. R. (1964) *The Preservation of Deteriorating Books: an examination of the problem with recommendations for a solution*, Washington, DC, Association of Research Libraries.

# Index

Page numbers in *italics* indicate references to figures.